WHAT'S FOR *Christmas* DINNER?

WHEN USING KITCHEN APPLIANCES PLEASE ALWAYS FOLLOW
THE MANUFACTURER'S INSTRUCTIONS

HarperCollins*Publishers*
1 London Bridge Street
London SE1 9GF

www.harpercollins.co.uk

HarperCollins*Publishers*
Macken House, 39/40 Mayor Street Upper
Dublin 1, D01 C9W8, Ireland

First published by HarperCollins*Publishers* 2024

13 5 7 9 10 8 6 4 2

Text © Sarah Rossi 2024
Photography © Sam Folan 2024

A catalogue record of this book is available from the British Library

ISBN 978-0-00-868559-1

Design by Lynnette Eve at Design Jam

Photographer: Sam Folan
Food Stylist: Pippa Leon
Prop Stylist: Lydia Brun

Printed and bound by GPS Group, Bosnia-Herzegovina

This book contains FSC™ certified paper and other controlled
sources to ensure responsible forest management.

For more information visit: www.harpercollins.co.uk/green

# WHAT'S FOR *Christmas* DINNER?

## Sarah Rossi

Festive Meal Plans, Big-Day Timings,
Essential Shopping Lists

HarperCollins*Publishers*

# CONTENTS

# Introduction

# WHAT'S FOR *Christmas* DINNER?

For the last decade, I've shared ideas online for how to eat well and feed your family during the week.

While an easy midweek meal is a definite win, on busy days there's not much time for indulging in the food that really makes peoples' eyes light up. That is where special occasion cooking comes in, and Christmas is the ultimate time for a table groaning with treats.

Whether your Christmas celebration is centred around religious beliefs or an annual time to come together with people you love, food is often a central part of these moments. It's a chance to share traditions and make memories to cherish.

If food is important to you during the festive season, you'll almost certainly have succumbed to food performance anxiety at some point. Over years of cooking at Christmas, especially with young children, the panic and exhaustion has set in many times for me personally. Years later, when I started to build a community online, I realised that this was a common shared experience.

This book contains everything I've learned about festive cooking, including my own successes (and failures!) and my very generous online audience sharing how their lives look over Christmas. This book is not just about the food, it's about how to enjoy the season and focus on what really matters (hint: it isn't whether your parsnips are crispy or not!).

Before we dive in, I'm conscious that this book refers to a very specific, very British Christmas, and the Christmas table won't look the same for everyone. This book also often refers to the type of celebration involving lots of people, and this may not be your situation or preference.

If this isn't your experience, I've created recipes that are easy to adapt, so you can find your own enjoyment in them, whatever Christmas is for you.

*Sarah*

# TOP TIPS FOR A STRESS-FREE *Festive* FOOD SEASON

## PLAN, PLAN, PLAN AHEAD

The festive intensity is real: gift shopping, wrapping, remembering the school play...
I hope that this book will help you make a plan for the food shopping and preparation so that
this element of your Christmas doesn't feel overwhelming, and allows you to enjoy the season.

## PREPARE EVERYTHING YOU CAN IN ADVANCE

Most of the recipes in this book are designed to be suitable for making in advance.
I find this approach to cooking over the festive season to be such a lifesaver. Getting ahead
leaves me to enjoy myself and relax when I really want to.

## USE DISPOSABLE FOIL TRAYS

I am not normally one for disposable items, as I try to avoid too much waste, but I have to say,
not washing up roasting pans when cooking a big meal really saves me.

## BUY AN EXTRA SHELF FOR YOUR OVEN

If your oven doesn't have 3 shelves and you're cooking a feast over the festive period,
you can buy a universal rack which sits just above the base of any size of oven.

## KEY TO RECIPES

 Vegetarian    Vegan    Vegan option

# STOCK UP

This is, it must be said, a very random list. It's the things that make my life easier during December, beyond our usual shopping for meals list, so I make sure to buy extra for the festive period. I hope it helps you too!

## HOUSEHOLD

- ☐ Tin foil
- ☐ Cling film
- ☐ Rubbish bags
- ☐ Rubber gloves
- ☐ Washing up liquid/dishwasher tablets
- ☐ Napkins
- ☐ Cellophane gift bags for homemade gifts
- ☐ Sellotape
- ☐ Batteries
- ☐ Candles for the table
- ☐ Electric rechargeable safe lighter
- ☐ Foil disposable roasting trays
- ☐ Foil trays to give away leftovers (the type with cardboard lids)
- ☐ A meat thermometer (it takes all of the guess work out of cooking meat, but particularly useful for turkey, which is easy to overcook)

## FOOD

- ☐ Bake-at-home bread (the type that lasts for ages and you bake in the oven – very handy when you don't have fresh bread for turkey sandwiches)
- ☐ Crackers (vital for cheese leftovers)
- ☐ Oven chips (for making a meal out of leftovers when you're really not in the mood for any more involved cooking)
- ☐ Baking potatoes (an extra bag of these for between Christmas and New Year)
- ☐ Pickles (onions/chutney – a given)
- ☐ Salad (the basics for sandwiches, lettuce, tomatoes, cucumber, etc.)

★

### A note on dietary requirements

I wanted to make this book as inclusive as possible, so that all of our guests can be welcome and enjoy food together. On pages 208–213, you'll find a table showing all of the recipes and which diets they are suitable for, along with suggestions on how to adapt them.

# ~Christmas Day~
## MENU

Classic Roast Turkey with Herb Butter *(p.32)*

Pigs in Blankets *(p.52)*

Stress-free Roast Potatoes *(p.54)*

Glazed Carrots & Parsnips *(p.58)*

Cauliflower Cheese *(p.62)*

Braised Red Cabbage *(p.61)*

Festive Brussels Sprouts *(p.60)*

Sausage & Apricot Stuffing *(p.66)*

Make-ahead Gravy *(p.70)*

# Christmas Day MENU
## SHOPPING LIST

I have multiplied the recipe amounts here to give you options if you're cooking for a large group.

| FRUIT & VEG | FOR 6 | FOR 8 | FOR 12 |
|---|---|---|---|
| Parsnips | ☐ 750g | ☐ 1kg | ☐ 1.5kg |
| Carrots | ☐ 750g | ☐ 1kg | ☐ 1.5kg |
| Brussels sprouts | ☐ 750g | ☐ 1kg | ☐ 1.5kg |
| Cauliflower | ☐ 700g | ☐ 1kg | ☐ 1.5kg |
| White potatoes | ☐ 1.5kg | ☐ 2kg | ☐ 3kg |
| Onions | ☐ 1 | ☐ 2 | ☐ 2 |
| Oranges | ☐ 1 | ☐ 1 | ☐ 2 |
| Lemons | ☐ 2 | ☐ 2 | ☐ 3 |
| Fresh thyme | ☐ 20g | ☐ 20g | ☐ 25g |
| Fresh rosemary | ☐ 20g | ☐ 20g | ☐ 25g |
| Fresh sage | ☐ 10g | ☐ 15g | ☐ 20g |

*I like Maris Piper or King Edward*

| MEAT & FISH | | | |
|---|---|---|---|
| Turkey or equivalent turkey crown | ☐ 4kg | ☐ 4kg | ☐ 5kg |
| Streaky bacon | ☐ 370g | ☐ 410g | ☐ 550g |
| Diced pancetta or bacon lardons | ☐ 200g | ☐ 265g | ☐ 400g |
| Chipolata sausages | ☐ 12 | ☐ 16 | ☐ 24 |
| Pork sausages | ☐ 450g (about 8) | ☐ 600g (about 10) | ☐ 900g (about 16) |

| FRIDGE/FREEZER | | | |
|---|---|---|---|
| Milk (semi-skimmed or whole) | ☐ 500ml | ☐ 650ml | ☐ 1 litre |
| Salted butter | ☐ 275g | ☐ 280g | ☐ 365g |
| Parmesan cheese | ☐ 150g | ☐ 210g | ☐ 300g |
| Red Leicester cheese | ☐ 125g | ☐ 165g | ☐ 250g |

| EVERYTHING ELSE | | | |
|---|---|---|---|
| Cooked chestnuts | ☐ 240g | ☐ 320g | ☐ 480g |
| Dried apricots | ☐ 50g | ☐ 70g | ☐ 100g |

*The type in a vacuum pack*

## STORE CUPBOARD
- ☐ Sea salt
- ☐ Freshly ground black pepper
- ☐ Sunflower oil
- ☐ Onion granules
- ☐ Garlic granules
- ☐ Dried thyme
- ☐ Runny honey
- ☐ Cornflour
- ☐ Dijon mustard
- ☐ Breadcrumbs

*I like Panko*

The shopping list doesn't include ingredients for Braised Red Cabbage or Make-ahead Gravy as you will have frozen these in advance.

# Christmas Day MENU PREPARATION PLAN

This is the schedule I use to keep me cool, calm and collected to serve the Christmas Day menu (on page 13) on 25th December. You can adjust this to suit your own menu. Each recipe includes make ahead instructions. (You can freeze some components in advance if you'd like to be even more organised. There are options for this on the individual recipes where relevant.)

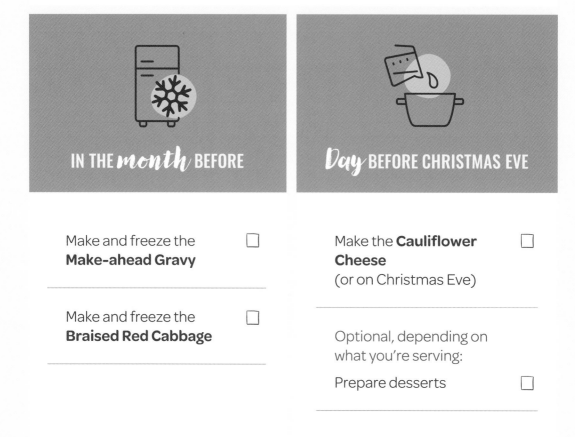

### IN THE *month* BEFORE

Make and freeze the **Make-ahead Gravy** ☐

Make and freeze the **Braised Red Cabbage** ☐

### *Day* BEFORE CHRISTMAS EVE

Make the **Cauliflower Cheese** (or on Christmas Eve) ☐

Optional, depending on what you're serving:

Prepare desserts ☐

# *Christmas Eve* TO DO LIST

Take the **Braised Red Cabbage** out of freezer to defrost ☐

Take the **Make-ahead Gravy** out of freezer to defrost ☐

Make the **Herb Butter** for the turkey and prep the turkey (15 minutes) ☐

Part-cook the **Festive Brussels Sprouts** ingredients (10 minutes) ☐

Make the **Sausage & Apricot Stuffing** (15 minutes) ☐

Part-cook the **Stress-free Roast Potatoes**
(15 minutes prep + 45 minutes bake) ☐

Part-cook the **Glazed Carrots & Parsnips**
(10 minutes prep + 30 minutes bake) ☐

Part-cook the **Pigs in Blankets** (10 minutes prep + 20 minutes bake) ☐

Optional, depending on what you're serving:

Prepare nibbles ☐

Prepare desserts ☐

Prepare breakfast for tomorrow ☐

# Christmas Day

The timings overleaf assume that you've done the pre-cooking mentioned opposite and that your oven has three shelves (if it doesn't, buy an extra shelf to sit on the floor of your oven!). You will have...

## PART-COOKED

Stress-free Roast Potatoes ☐

Glazed Carrots & Parsnips ☐

Festive Brussels Sprouts ☐

Pigs in Blankets ☐

## MADE AND DEFROSTED

Braised Red Cabbage ☐

Make-ahead Gravy ☐

## PREPARED AND CHILLED

Cauliflower Cheese ☐

## PLUS

Optional nibbles ☐

Optional desserts ☐

# Christmas Day
## TIMINGS

The timings below assume that you've done the pre-cooking mentioned in the preparation plan and that your oven has three shelves (if it doesn't, buy an extra shelf to sit on the floor of your oven!)

| | | |
|---|---|---|
| *7:00* | Take the turkey out of the fridge | ☐ |
| *8:00* | Turkey in (this will depend on the size of your turkey: work backwards so it is ready to serve at 13:00 and adjust the starting time accordingly) | ☐ |
| *10:15* | Optional: Prepare and cook Slow Cooker Chocolate Orange Pudding | ☐ |
| *12:00* | Turkey out (to rest for 1 hour) | ☐ |
| | Sausage & Apricot Stuffing in | ☐ |
| | Finish off nibbles and desserts | ☐ |
| *12:15* | Cauliflower Cheese in | ☐ |
| *12:30* | Roast Potatoes in | ☐ |
| *12:45* | Sausage & Apricot Stuffing out (cover with foil to keep warm) | ☐ |
| | Cauliflower Cheese out (cover with foil to keep warm) | ☐ |
| | Glazed Carrots & Parsnips in | ☐ |
| | Pigs in Blankets in | ☐ |
| | Festive Brussels Sprouts reheat on the hob | ☐ |
| | Braised Red Cabbage reheat on the hob | ☐ |
| | Make-ahead Gravy reheat on the hob | ☐ |
| *13:00* | Check everything is ready, enjoy! | ☐ |

# Christmas Day
## TIMINGS

Here is a blank time plan in case the timings on the opposite page don't suit your day. Feel free to use mine as a guide and create your own here.

| Time | | |
|------|---|---|
| | | ☐ |
| | | ☐ |
| | | ☐ |
| | | ☐ |
| | | ☐ |
| | | ☐ |
| | | ☐ |
| | | ☐ |
| | | ☐ |
| | | ☐ |
| | | ☐ |
| | | ☐ |
| | | ☐ |
| | | ☐ |

# WHAT'S COOKING WHERE

One of the biggest juggles of cooking a meal with so many dishes is oven space. This plan aims to simplify this by showing how to fit everything in. These timings assume that your oven has three shelves (read more about this on page 19).

| | 180°c | | 200°c | |
|---|---|---|---|---|
| **Classic Roast Turkey with Herb Butter** | Out to rest – 1 hour | | | |
| **Sausage & Apricot Stuffing** | 45 minutes – Middle oven shelf | | | |
| **Cauliflower Cheese** | | 30 minutes – Bottom oven shelf | | |
| **Stress-free Roast Potatoes** | | | 30 minutes – Top oven shelf | |
| **Glazed Carrots & Parsnips** | | | | 15 minutes Middle oven shelf |
| **Pigs in Blankets** | | | | 15 minutes – Bottom oven shelf |
| **Festive Brussels Sprouts** | | | | 15 minutes Hob |
| **Braised Red Cabbage** | | | | 15 minutes Hob |
| **Make-ahead Gravy** | | | | 15 minutes Hob |

12:00    12:15    12:30    12:45    13:00

# ~Christmas Day~

## VEGETARIAN MENU

Mushroom Wellingtons *(p.42)*

Stress-free Roast Potatoes *(p.54)*

Glazed Carrots & Parsnips *(p.58)*

Cauliflower Cheese *(p.62)*
(use adaptions from page 209)

Braised Red Cabbage *(p.61)*

Festive Brussels Sprouts *(p.60)*

Sage & Onion Stuffing Balls *(p.68)*

Make-ahead Gravy *(p.70)*

## VEGAN MENU

Ridiculously Delicious Nut Roast *(p.46)*

Stress-free Roast Potatoes *(p.54)*

Glazed Carrots & Parsnips *(p.58)*

Braised Red Cabbage *(p.61)*

Sage & Onion Stuffing Balls *(p.68)*

Make-ahead Gravy *(p.70)*

# BREAKFAST MENU

Hash Brown Breakfast Bake *(p.102)*

Christmas Tree Fruit Salad *(p.100)*

Croissant Christmas Tree *(p.94)*

Christmas Morning Cocktail Cubes *(p.104)*

# BUFFET PARTY MENU

Slow Cooker Roasted Gammon *(p.108)*

Cheese & Tomato Tart *(p.116)*

Caprese-style Pasta Salad *(p.120)*

Roasted Winter Salad *(p.118)*

Christmas Coleslaw *(p.122)*

For gluten-free, dairy-free and nut-free diets, you will find easy adaptions for many recipes at the back of this book (see pages 208–213).

# Festive Feast

This is it, the big day!

In this chapter you'll find a one-stop-shop for how to make your Christmas Day as smooth as possible and reduce overwhelm, leaving you to enjoy the festivities.

My tactic is always to make everything we can in advance, even part-cooking some dishes to avoid the oven space juggle.

I've included timings and a shopping list for the classic Christmas dinner (see pages 14–22), though of course you can adjust this, make your own menu and use my time plans as a guide.

# CLASSIC ROAST TURKEY WITH HERB BUTTER

**3 HOURS 20 MINS, PLUS RESTING TIME (BASED ON A 4KG TURKEY)**

Roast Turkey is, without a doubt, the pinnacle of a traditional British Christmas meal. Ever the trendsetter, it was Queen Victoria serving it for Christmas in 1851 (alongside goose and beef) that made it the meat of choice for 25th December from then on. Despite roast turkey having been traditional for almost two centuries, the thought of cooking one is often enough to bring even a confident cook out in a panic. But this method here is foolproof, and very well tried and tested – it is the product of many turkey fails: I have undercooked it, overcooked it, and even tried cooking it on the barbecue! (That's another story.)

If you're planning to cook a whole turkey (or a turkey crown) this Christmas, this recipe and advice (see pages 34–35 for lots of useful tips) will give you a helping hand to make it your best yet.

1. **Remove the turkey from the fridge and set aside. Put the herb butter ingredients in a bowl and mash together well.**

2. **Remove the giblets (if your turkey has them) and put the turkey into a well-lined roasting tin or a foil tray placed on a baking tray (to support it). Pat the turkey dry with kitchen towel, then use a small, sharp knife to gently part the skin from the breasts at the highest point. Using a clean hand, separate the skin from the meat. Repeat on the other side of the bird too.**

3. **Push about half of the herb butter under the skin of the turkey. You can use your hands on top of the skin to help push it down. Spread the rest of the butter over the top of the skin. Lay the bacon rashers carefully over the turkey breast (I like to criss-cross them as this helps to stop them falling off as they cook). Cover loosely with foil.**

4. **When you're ready to cook, preheat the oven to 180°C fan/200°C/Gas Mark 6 and cook according to the timings on page 35 (or on the turkey packaging), basing the cooking time on its weight.**

5. **Baste the turkey every hour or so. If, an hour before the end of the cooking time, the outside of the turkey or the bacon are not turning brown, remove the foil to allow for a crispy finish.**

6. **When the turkey is cooked through, remove it from the oven but leave it in its tray (lots of juice will come out).** »

## SERVES 6–8

**4kg** whole turkey or turkey crown
**250g** smoked streaky bacon rashers

**For the Herb Butter**
**250g** salted butter,
  at room temperature
**20g** fresh thyme, leaves removed
  from stalks and finely chopped
**20g** fresh rosemary, leaves removed
  from stalks and finely chopped
**2** lemons, zested
**1** orange, zested
plenty of sea salt and freshly
  ground black pepper

## TO MAKE AHEAD

Prep up to the end of step 3 up to 24 hours before you're ready to cook the turkey. Cover and chill it overnight, then cook as normal in the morning. A fridge-cold turkey may take a little longer to cook than a room temperature one.

Set aside somewhere not too chilly in the kitchen and keep it covered with foil. Pop a clean bath towel or a couple of clean tea towels on top of the foil to keep the heat in and let it rest for about 1 hour.

7. When you're ready to serve, pour the resting juices from the tray into your gravy (if you wish). Place the turkey on a platter and carve.

# HOW TO COOK YOUR BEST TURKEY EVER

The following tips and advice refer to cooking a whole turkey. If you prefer to use a turkey crown (legs removed) or a boneless turkey crown, you will need to adjust the serving sizes and cooking times accordingly.

## WHAT SIZE TO BUY
According to Copas Turkeys:

| WEIGHT | SERVES (PEOPLE) |
|--------|-----------------|
| 4kg | 8–10 |
| 5kg | 10–12 |
| 6kg | 12–14 |
| 7kg | 14–16 |
| 8kg | 16–18 |
| 9kg | 18–20 |

## THAWING A FROZEN TURKEY

Plan this well in advance! Turkeys are hefty birds and take some thawing out – large ones can take up to 5 days. If you are cooking a frozen turkey, check the packet instructions well beforehand, as most do need to be defrosted.

According to official guidance from the UK Food Standards Agency, you should always defrost your turkey in the fridge rather than at room temperature. You'll need to put it in a container too, in case any liquid comes out (to avoid cross-contamination and a messy fridge).

If you don't have thawing instructions, allow 10–12 hours per kg for a complete thaw.

## TAKE OUT THE GIBLETS

These are the innards of the turkey and they are usually inside the bird in a bag, so you just need to remove the bag before you roast the turkey. You don't need them for your turkey, but they're great for additional flavour in your gravy if you want to go the extra mile.

## JUST BEFORE COOKING

Remove the turkey from the fridge and leave it at room temperature for about an hour before you're going to cook it. This stops it from shrinking in the hot oven and helps it cook evenly.

## FOIL

I like to cook the turkey covered in foil, to make sure that it is not cooking too quickly. If, an hour before the end of the cooking time, the outside of the turkey or the bacon are not yet turning brown, take off the foil to allow a crispy finish.

## BASTING

Basting the meat with the cooking liquid helps to stop it drying out. Be aware that if you open the oven door often, the turkey may take longer to cook as the heat escapes. Always check it is fully cooked before serving.

## BACON

I use the bacon to add flavour and keep the turkey breasts tender. By the time the bird has cooked, the bacon can be a little overcooked and hard so discard it if you like, but we always eat it crumbled over the meat!

## COOKING TIME

Weigh the turkey first so you get your timings correct.

According to the UK Food Standards Agency, you should follow these guidelines:

| WEIGHT | TIMINGS |
|---|---|
| under 4.5kg | 45 minutes per kg, plus 20 minutes |
| 4.5–6.5kg | 40 minutes per kg |
| over 6.5kg | 35 minutes per kg |

## HOW TO CHECK IT'S COOKED

A meat thermometer is the best way to check meat, particularly turkey, is cooked (I like the Thermapen brand). Always check the thickest part of the meat (usually the thigh). It will be ready when the temperature is either:

| | |
|---|---|
| 65°C | for 10 minutes |
| 70°C | for 2 minutes |
| 75°C | for 30 seconds |

# SLOW COOKER
# TURKEY & GRAVY

**3 HOURS 15 MINS, PLUS RESTING TIME**

If you want to serve turkey but don't fancy handling an unwieldy whole bird – or don't have enough oven space – here's the option for you. Cooking it this way gives the turkey plenty of flavour, while also keeping it very tender.

   As always, for the best results, use a meat thermometer if you can, and especially here as slow cookers can vary so much. When your turkey reaches the correct internal temperature (see page 35) you'll know it's done – no overcooking here!

1. Put all of the ingredients into the slow cooker, put the lid on and cook on HIGH for 2½–3½ hours or LOW for 4–5 hours.

2. When the turkey is cooked, remove it from the slow cooker and put it onto a plate, cover tightly with foil and put a clean hand towel, folded so it's double thickness, on top of the foil. (This will keep the meat warm.)

3. Sit a sieve on top of a large jug or mixing bowl and pour the liquid from the slow cooker through this. Discard the bits in the sieve (including the bay leaves) and return the liquid to the slow cooker (or saucepan, see below).

4. Put the cornflour in a small bowl (don't skip this step, it's important otherwise the gravy will be lumpy!), add the soy sauce and a teaspoon of the cooking liquid and mix it until it forms a very smooth paste. You may need another teaspoon (or even two) of the cooking liquid. Add this paste to the rest of the liquid in the slow cooker (or saucepan, see below).

5. Now either, cook the gravy in the slow cooker: put the lid on the slow cooker and cook on HIGH for 30 minutes, whisking every 5 minutes or so to avoid lumps forming.
OR
Cook the gravy in a saucepan over a medium heat for 5–10 minutes until thickened. (I recommend this method, as it is less likely to become lumpy, it's quicker, and you won't scratch a metal slow cooker with your whisk! However, use the slow cooker if you won't have space on the hob.)

6. Slice the turkey thinly and serve with the gravy.

## SERVES 6

**1.5kg** turkey breast (or boneless, skinless turkey crown as it's sometimes called)
**450ml** hot chicken stock (made from a cube is fine)
**2 tsp** onion granules
**2 tsp** garlic granules
**2 tsp** dried thyme
**3** bay leaves
sea salt and freshly ground black pepper

### For the Gravy
**40g** cornflour
**2 tbsp** dark soy sauce (I use reduced salt)

## TO MAKE WITHOUT A SLOW COOKER

Use 700ml of stock rather than 450ml. Simmer in a casserole dish over a medium heat for about 45–60 minutes or until the meat is cooked through. Finish by making the gravy as instructed opposite.

# SLOW COOKER
# ROAST BEEF

## 5 HOURS 25 MINUTES

If beef is your meat of choice on Christmas Day, this hands-off method of cooking it will produce a tender, slow-cooked joint. The added bonus is the rich and thick gravy that it makes as it cooks. If you want to cook a larger beef joint, just adjust the cooking time and be sure it fits into your slow cooker!

1. Sprinkle the flour, thyme, garlic granules and salt and pepper on a chopping board. Dry the beef well with kitchen paper, then roll in the flour mixture to coat it all over.

2. Heat the oil in a large frying pan over a high heat, or if your slow cooker allows it, by putting the slow cooker dish on the hob. Brown the meat on all sides until golden.

3. Remove the meat from the pan and set aside, add the garlic, onions and carrots to the pan and cook for about 5–10 minutes until they start to soften. If you're using your slow cooker dish, add the meat back in. If you're using a frying pan, transfer everything to your slow cooker dish. Pour in the stock, pop the lid on and cook on HIGH for 5–6 hours or LOW for 7–8 hours until the meat is tender.

4. When cooked, transfer the meat to a serving dish, reserving the cooking liquid.

5. To make the gravy, put the cornflour in a small bowl (don't skip this step, it's important otherwise the gravy will be lumpy!) and spoon in enough of the cooking liquid to form a smooth paste. Add this paste back to the rest of the liquid in the slow cooker (or saucepan, see below).

6. Now either, cook the gravy in the slow cooker: put the lid on and cook on HIGH for 30 minutes, whisking every 5 minutes or so to avoid lumps forming.
   OR
   Cook the gravy in a saucepan over a medium heat for 5–10 minutes until thickened. (I recommend this method, as it is less likely to become lumpy, it's quicker, and you won't scratch a metal slow cooker with your whisk! However, use the slow cooker if you won't have space on the hob.)

7. Slice the beef and serve with the gravy and vegetables.

### SERVES 6

**2 tbsp** plain flour
**1 tbsp** dried thyme
**1 tbsp** garlic granules
**1.5kg** beef topside joint
**1 tbsp** olive oil
**3** garlic cloves, peeled and chopped or crushed
**2** onions, peeled and quartered
**3** carrots, peeled and quartered
**400ml** hot beef stock (made from a cube is fine)
**3 tbsp** cornflour, for the gravy
sea salt and freshly ground black pepper

### TO MAKE WITHOUT A SLOW COOKER

In step 3, put the browned meat and softened vegetables, along with the stock, into a lidded casserole dish and bake at 160°C for 2½–3 hours until the meat is very tender. When cooked, carefully remove the meat and vegetables, cover and set aside. Mix the cornflour with a little cold water to make a smooth paste, add back to the cooking liquid and continue as per the saucepan gravy option at step 5.

# MUSHROOM WELLINGTONS

V

**1 HOUR 50 MINS**

This vegetarian main course includes a whole bulb of garlic: yes, you read that right! The garlic slow roasts with the mushrooms, making the most delicious creamy filling, which feels utterly decadent and perfectly suitable for a special meal. The cooking time here is reasonably long, but it is really worth it, and it can all be done in advance. This recipe serves four, but it can easily be halved or doubled depending on how many vegetarians are dining.

1. Preheat the oven to 180°C fan/200°C/Gas Mark 6.

2. **Trim the very top off the garlic bulb and sit it on a small piece of foil.**

3. **Put the mushrooms on a baking tray, stalks facing up, drizzle the olive oil over the mushrooms and garlic, and season with salt and pepper. Wrap the garlic up in the foil and sit it on the tray next to the mushrooms.**

4. **In a separate ovenproof dish, add the leeks, thyme and butter. Cover tightly with foil (or a lid if your dish has one).**

5. **Put the mushroom tray and leek dish in the oven and set a timer for 30 minutes.**

6. **When the timer goes off, remove the mushroom tray from the oven (leave the leek dish in there) and carefully drain off any liquid from the mushrooms. Turn the mushrooms over then cook both the leeks, and mushrooms and garlic (still in separate dishes), for another 30 minutes.**

7. **Remove the leeks, mushrooms and garlic from the oven and allow to cool.**

8. **Assemble the wellingtons: when the leeks are cold, take the garlic bulb and squeeze the contents out of the papery skin into the leeks in a bowl. Add the cream cheese and a good seasoning of salt and pepper. Mix well, mashing the garlic, until completely combined.** »

## SERVES 4

**1** garlic bulb
**8** portobello mushrooms
 (2 per person)
**1 tbsp** olive oil
**2** leeks, halved, washed and
 cut into 5mm-thick slices
**10g** fresh thyme, leaves removed
 from stalks
**30g** salted butter
**200g** garlic and herb cream cheese
**640g** ready-rolled puff pastry
 (2 x 320g packs)
**1** egg, beaten
sea salt and freshly ground
 black pepper

### TO MAKE AHEAD

Prepare up to step 11, but don't bake. Store in the fridge on the baking tray, covered, for up to 24 hours until you are ready to cook.

# MUSHROOM WELLINGTONS

**1 HOUR 50 MINS**

9. Unroll the sheet of puff pastry and use a sharp knife to cut it into thirds, cutting across the width of the pastry not the length (see Note). Taking one pastry third at a time, position a mushroom at the end of the pastry, add a quarter of the leek and cream cheese mixture, then put another mushroom on top. Repeat for all 4 mushrooms.

10. Use a pastry brush to brush the beaten egg around each mushroom.

11. Fold the pastry over the top of each mushroom and use a fork to press the edges of the pastry together. (Use clean hands to smooth the pastry gently over the upturned mushroom.) Cut around the mushroom parcels in a circular shape. Brush the top of the pastry with the remaining egg and use the pastry offcuts to decorate, if you like.

12. Bake in the oven on a lined baking tray for 25–30 minutes until the pastry is golden.

> ★
>
> Annoyingly, 1 sheet of puff pastry is enough for 3 mushrooms, so you will need 1 sheet plus an extra third of a sheet for 4 mushrooms. You can freeze the leftover pastry for another time, however, or make my Puff Pastry Mince Pie Swirls (see page 200), so it won't go to waste!

# RIDICULOUSLY DELICIOUS NUT ROAST

**1 HOUR 30 MINS**

I need to shout from the rooftops how good this recipe is, because whether you're vegan, vegetarian or a loyal turkey eater, it makes an utterly delicious centrepiece. If you're a Marmite hater, please don't be put off, it just adds a savoury intensity. Be sure to chop your nuts quite finely (I use a mini food processor), as it gives the best texture for slicing the loaf without it crumbling.

1. **Preheat oven to 180°C fan/200°C/Gas Mark 6 and line the loaf tin with baking paper, making sure the paper overhangs the edges of the tin so you can use this later to lift the roast out. Grease any parts of the tin not covered in paper with oil.**

2. **Cook the sweet potato slices in a small saucepan of boiling salted water for 7–8 minutes until softened but not breaking up. Drain and set aside.**

3. **Heat the oil in a medium saucepan over a low-medium heat, add the onion and cook for 5 minutes or until starting to soften, then add the sage and cook for a further 5 minutes until the onions are soft but not coloured. Remove the pan from the heat.**

4. **Mix the boiling water in a heatproof bowl with the stock cube until it has dissolved, add the breadcrumbs and stir well. Set aside for at least 5 minutes.**

5. **Reserve half of the sweet potato slices and set aside. Mash the remaining half well.**

6. **To the onion and sage, add the mixed nuts, tomato purée, Marmite, cranberry sauce, soaked breadcrumbs, mashed sweet potatoes and plenty of salt and pepper. Mix very well.**

7. **Sprinkle pistachios over the base of the tin. Add half the nut mixture and press down firmly. Arrange the remaining slices of sweet potato in a neat layer (you will need to overlap and/or trim them), then pile on the remaining nut mixture and press very firmly.**

8. **Bake in the oven for 40–50 minutes, or until the top is starting to turn dark brown and the loaf feels springy.**

9. **Remove from the oven and leave to stand for 10 minutes before turning out, using the baking paper to help you. Carefully cut into slices to serve.**

## SERVES 6

**400g** sweet potatoes (about 2), peeled and cut into 5mm-thick slices
**2 tbsp** olive oil, plus extra for greasing
**1** onion, peeled and very finely chopped
**15g** sage leaves, finely chopped
**150ml** boiling water
**1** vegetable stock cube (undiluted)
**50g** breadcrumbs (such as panko)
**300g** unsalted mixed nuts, very finely chopped
**2 tbsp** tomato purée
**1 tbsp** Marmite
**100g** cranberry sauce (shop-bought or see page 72)
**50g** shelled unsalted pistachios
sea salt and freshly ground black pepper

**You will need:** 900g (2lb) loaf tin

### TO MAKE AHEAD

Prepare up to the end of step 7 and store the pressed mixture in the fridge for up to 24 hours until you are ready to bake. The loaf may take extra time to cook if it's cold from the fridge. Ensure it's hot through in the centre before serving.

# ORANGE & HONEY GLAZED SALMON

**40 MINS**

This recipe is a show-stopping fish centrepiece for Christmas Day, or a buffet meal. A whole side of salmon coated in a simple but festive glaze, which adds colour and flavour. I like to lay the orange pieces along the middle of the fish as decoration, in slightly kitsch 80s fashion, a throwback to Christmases of my childhood.

1. **Preheat the oven to 180°C fan/200°C/Gas Mark 6.**

2. **Mix the orange zest (save the fruit for later), 2 tablespoons of honey, ginger, garlic granules and plenty of salt and pepper into a paste.**

3. **Sit the salmon skin side down onto two sheets of overlapping foil (you need to be able to fold them up to make a sealed parcel all around the fish). Pat the fish dry with kitchen paper. Smear the paste onto the top of the salmon (try to keep most of it in the middle so it doesn't run down the edges as it cooks).**

4. **Cut the zested orange into thin slices and sit on top of the salmon. Seal the foil around the fish and bake in the oven for 30–40 minutes, or until the fish is cooked through.**

5. **Before serving, drizzle the honey over the orange slices.**

## SERVES 6

1 orange, zested
2 **tbsp** runny honey, plus an extra **1 tbsp** to finish
2 **tsp** ground ginger
2 **tsp** garlic granules
**1kg** side of salmon
sea salt and freshly ground black pepper

## TO MAKE AHEAD

Prepare the paste and set aside. Only smear it onto the fish just before baking or the citrus can start to 'cook' the salmon a little.

# ROAST TURKEY TRAYBAKE

## 1 HOUR

If you're looking for a more low-key Christmas dinner but still want to enjoy festive flavours, this traybake recipe is a delicious option. Everything is cooked together, reducing washing up and timing stresses. This recipe is also ideal if you're cooking for two people: you could halve the ingredients listed or make it as below and enjoy leftovers later.

1. **Preheat the oven to 180°C fan/200°C/Gas Mark 6.**

2. **Put 2 tablespoons of the olive oil in a large bowl with the onion granules, garlic granules and sage and mix well. Add the carrots and potatoes and toss in the oil until everything is well coated.**

3. **Tip the potatoes and carrots onto 2 baking trays and spread them out evenly. (Put the empty bowl to one side and don't wash it up – we'll use it later.)**

4. **Roast the potatoes and carrots in the oven for 20 minutes, or until starting to brown at the edges.**

5. **To make the turkey parcels, squeeze the sausage meat from the skins into another bowl (to do this, I cut along the long edge of each sausage and then turn them inside out). Discard the skins. Add the cranberry sauce and dried sage to the sausages, along with plenty of salt and pepper, and mash well until combined.**

6. **Now take either 1 large or 2 small turkey pieces and lay them flat (this will depend on the cut of the fillets in your pack as they can vary a lot – just work out so you have 4 even portions of about 200g each). Pat dry with kitchen paper.**

7. **Spoon a quarter of the sausage mixture onto the middle and roll the turkey up. Secure each parcel with 3 rashers of streaky bacon. (You can use a cocktail stick to hold them together if they are a little slippery.) Smear the butter over the top of the turkey parcels in small pats.**

8. **Put the sprouts in the bowl from earlier, add the remaining tablespoon of olive oil and plenty of salt and pepper and mix well to coat. Set aside.**

9. **When the timer for the potatoes and carrots goes off, remove the trays from the oven and add the sprouts.** »

### SERVES 4

**For the Vegetables**
**3 tbsp** olive oil
**2 tsp** onion granules
**2 tsp** garlic granules
**1 tsp** dried sage
**400g** Chantenay carrots
**4** baking potatoes, cut into 3cm cubes, peeling optional (about 800g)
**500g** Brussels sprouts, trimmed (about 340g trimmed weight)

**For the Turkey Parcels**
**250g** pork sausages (about 4)
**30g** cranberry sauce (shop-bought or see page 72)
**1 tsp** dried sage
**2 x 400g** packs turkey steaks (about 8 steaks)
**12** rashers of streaky bacon (about 250g)
**60g** salted butter, at room temperature
sea salt and freshly ground black pepper

### TO MAKE AHEAD

Prepare the turkey parcels and store, covered in the fridge, for up to 24 hours before cooking with the rest of the traybake.

Gently move the vegetables to one side and place your turkey steaks next to them on to the tray.

10. Roast for a further 30–35 minutes until the vegetables have softened, the turkey is cooked through and the bacon starting to crisp.

# PIGS IN BLANKETS

**30 MINS**

What would roast turkey be without these bacon-wrapped sausages served on the side? Of course, you can buy these ready-rolled in the supermarket if you prefer but I am quite happy to roll these myself on Christmas Eve to make sure each one gets a full quota of bacon!

1. **Preheat the oven to 180°C fan/200°C/Gas Mark 6.**

2. **Brush or wipe the base of a baking tray with the oil – the sausages will release some fat as they cook but this helps them not to stick initially.**

3. **Using scissors, cut each piece of streaky bacon in half, so you end up with two shorter pieces. Wrap each sausage in a piece of streaky bacon.**

4. **Put the wrapped sausages on the baking tray and bake for 25–30 minutes or until browned and cooked through.**

### SERVES 6

**1 tsp** sunflower oil
**12** chipolata sausages
**120g** streaky bacon (6 rashers), smoked or unsmoked (whichever you prefer)

### TO MAKE AHEAD

Cook as per step 4, but for only 20 minutes. Cool, cover and store in the fridge.

The next day finish cooking by baking in the hot oven for 10–15 minutes. (They will take a little longer than the total time above, as they have been cold in the fridge.) Ensure that they are golden brown and cooked through before serving.

# STRESS-FREE ROAST POTATOES

**VG**

---

## 1 HOUR 30 MINS

Is there any joy in life like the joy of a hot, crunchy, golden roast potato? Much as I love them dearly, I have always found cooking them to be the thing that may tip me slightly into the realms of Christmas lunch chaos. They tend to be somewhat unpredictable in their cooking time, mostly because we are opening and closing the oven door so much. Here is my tried and tested method to make them stress free, with options to part-cook them ahead of time.

1. **Preheat the oven to 200°C fan/220°C/Gas Mark 7.**

2. **Put the potatoes into a saucepan of cold salted water, pop on the lid, bring to the boil and cook for 10 minutes, until just starting to soften.**

3. **Meanwhile, pour 60ml (about 4 tablespoons) of the oil into a large roasting tray (or disposable foil tray) and place in the oven to heat up.**

4. **Drain the potatoes and put them back into the hot saucepan to dry for about 5 minutes.**

5. **Add the remaining oil to the potatoes, along with the onion granules and sea salt. Put the lid back on the pan and give them a really good shake.**

6. **Carefully tip the potatoes into the hot oil in the tray. The oil should be so hot that when you drop the first potato in you can hear it bubbling. Toss quickly until they are well coated (so the oil doesn't have time to cool) and roast in the oven for about 1 hour until golden and crispy all over (I always allow at least 1 hour 15 minutes).**

| SERVES 6 |
|---|

**1.5kg** white potatoes (I like Maris Piper, or King Edward), peeled and cut in half or thirds
**150ml** sunflower oil
**1 tbsp** onion granules
**½ tsp** sea salt

### The day before (WITH part-baking)

Follow the method, but only roast for
45 minutes–1 hour. They should be almost done
but not quite crispy enough to serve. Leave to
cool, cover and place in the fridge overnight.

To finish them off the following day, cook for
15–30 minutes until golden and crispy
(this can take a while as the potatoes will be
cold from the fridge).

### The day before (WITHOUT part-baking)

Follow the method until the end of step 5
(do not heat the oil at step 3). Leave to cool,
cover and place in the fridge until you're ready
to roast. Heat the oil as per step 3 and follow
the rest of the method.

### Making ahead TO FREEZE
### (no part-bake)

Follow the method until
step 5 (do not heat the oil at step 3).
Put the potatoes on a tray lined with
baking paper and freeze uncovered,
making sure the potatoes are not
touching for at least 1 hour. Once they
have hardened, you can transfer them
to a freezer-safe container (this extra
step might seem annoying but it stops
the potatoes sticking together). You
can keep them frozen for up to 1 month.
Defrost them overnight in the fridge, heat
the oil as per step 3 and follow the
rest of the method.

# ROAST POTATO TIPS

Shape: I like to cut the potatoes lengthways as this gives one lovely
flat crispy side as there's more surface area to touch the pan.

Cooking time: Keep an eye on your potatoes when they're boiling as if they are cut a bit
smaller, they may take less than 10 minutes' boiling time – they shouldn't start to fall apart.

If you're cooking the potatoes after they've been in the fridge, the cooking time may be a
little longer than normal, as the potatoes will be cold.

If you are cooking a whole roast dinner and opening the oven door a lot,
you may find your roasties take a little longer.

STRESS-FREE
ROAST POTATOES
p.54

# GLAZED CARROTS & PARSNIPS

**50 MINS**

This is a favourite festive side dish for me, not just because it tastes delicious, but also because one oven tray is delivering two different vegetables – that's the kind of side-dish efficiency we need for this busy meal. I always like to make an extra-large portion, as leftovers work very well in Boxing Day Pie on page 136 and Boxing Day Frittata on page 140.

1. **Preheat the oven to 180°C fan/200°C/Gas Mark 6 and line a baking tray with baking paper (or use a disposable foil tray).**

2. **Put the vegetables in a large bowl with the oil, half of the honey or maple syrup, all the thyme and plenty of salt and pepper. Toss until everything is coated, then place in a single layer on the lined tray and roast in the oven for 20 minutes.**

3. **Turn the vegetables over and roast for a further 20 minutes until sticky and tender.**

4. **Remove from the oven and drizzle with the remaining honey before serving.**

| SERVES 6 |
| --- |

**750g** parsnips, peeled and quartered
**750g** carrots, peeled and quartered
**4 tbsp** sunflower oil
**8 tbsp** runny honey (or maple syrup)
**4 tsp** dried thyme
sea salt and freshly ground
  black pepper

## TO MAKE AHEAD

### The day before (WITH part-roasting)

Roast for about 30 minutes, or until just colouring at the edges. Remove from the oven, leave to cool, then cover and store in the fridge. When you're ready to serve, roast for about 15 minutes to heat through and finish cooking. Drizzle with the remaining honey as above.

### The day before (WITHOUT part-roasting)

Follow the recipe to the point where you toss the veg in the honey, thyme and oil, and spread out on a lined baking tray. Cover and place in the fridge until you're ready to cook. When you're ready to serve, roast for about 40 minutes (turning halfway). Drizzle with the remaining honey as above.

### Making ahead to freeze (NO part-roasting)

Follow the recipe to the point where you toss the veg in the honey, thyme and oil, and spread out on a lined baking tray. Freeze uncovered, making sure they're not touching, for at least 1 hour (this stops them from sticking together). Once they're hard, transfer into a freezer-safe container and freeze for up to 1 month. When you're ready to serve, defrost and roast for about 40 minutes (turning halfway). Drizzle with the remaining honey as above.

# FESTIVE BRUSSELS SPROUTS

**15 MINS**

This is my mix-and-match method for perfect festive Brussels sprouts. In my own usual mode of festive indulgence, I like to include all three flavourings; crunchy fried pancetta for that deeply savoury edge, chestnuts for extra texture and Parmesan cheese (because what cannot be improved by cheese?). If you're not a fan of chestnuts or are cooking for vegetarians, mix and match as you prefer.

1. **Bring a saucepan of salted water to the boil. Plunge in the sprouts and cook for 5 minutes, then drain and transfer to a bowl of very cold water (don't skip this step – it stops them overcooking). Let them sit for 1 minute, then drain and set aside.**

2. **Heat a large frying pan or saucepan over a high heat and fry the pancetta until crispy.**

3. **Add the sprouts and chestnuts (if using) and fry for about 5 minutes until they are hot through and coated in the fat. Season with salt and pepper, and the Parmesan (if using).**

---

### SERVES 6

**750g** Brussels sprouts (unpeeled weight), peeled and trimmed
**200g** diced smoked pancetta (or smoked bacon lardons)
**150g** cooked chestnuts (the vacuum-packed type), roughly chopped (optional)
**50g** Parmesan cheese, grated (optional)
sea salt and freshly ground black pepper

---

### TO MAKE AHEAD

The day before, cook and cool the sprouts to the end of step 1. Fry the pancetta until crispy. Put the cold sprouts and the frying pan with the cooked pancetta, covered, in the fridge. When you're ready to cook, put the frying pan on the hob over a high heat, until the oil that the pancetta released is very hot. Add the cold sprouts and the chestnuts (if using) and pan-fry for about 5 minutes until they are hot through and coated in the oil. Top with Parmesan cheese (if using).

---

If you're not using pancetta, just fry the chestnuts in 2 tsp olive oil at step 2 for 2–3 minutes, then add the sprouts for a further 5 minutes.

# BRAISED RED CABBAGE

**2 HOURS 15 MINS**

This recipe makes 8 portions of this glistening, ruby-coloured side dish, which may be more than you need. But who wants to have half a leftover raw cabbage hanging around? Plus, if I'm cooking something for hours, it feels sensible to cook a larger portion. I always cook this in the early weeks of December and freeze it, so I have enough in the freezer for Christmas lunch and as a side dish on another day (perhaps to serve with Festive Beef Stew on page 110). If you want to halve the recipe, feel free, you'll just need to reduce the cooking time slightly. It's very important to include the red wine vinegar as this helps the cabbage to keep its beautiful purple colour.

1. **Preheat the oven to 140°C fan/160°C/Gas Mark 3.**

2. **Put all the ingredients, apart from the cranberry sauce and pomegranate seeds, in an ovenproof casserole dish and mix well. Cover and bake in the oven for 1½–2 hours until the cabbage is tender.**

3. **Just before serving, stir in the cranberry sauce and sprinkle with the pomegranate seeds.**

## TO MAKE WITH A SLOW COOKER

Put all the ingredients, apart from the cranberry sauce and pomegranate seeds, into the slow cooker and mix well. Pop on the lid and cook on HIGH for 2–3 hours or LOW for 4–5 hours, checking it occasionally to make sure that the cabbage doesn't overcook. When cooked, stir in the cranberry sauce and season with salt and pepper. Sprinkle over the pomegranate seeds to serve.

### SERVES 8

**1** red cabbage, cored and finely shredded
**2** red onions, peeled and cut into 3cm pieces
**3** cooking apples, peeled, cored and cut into 3cm pieces (about 600g)
**75g** soft dark brown sugar
**1 tbsp** mixed spice
**1 tsp** ground cinnamon
**75g** unsalted butter
**3 tbsp** red wine vinegar
**100g** cranberry sauce (shop-bought or see page 72)
sea salt and freshly ground black pepper

**To Serve**
**80g** pomegranate seeds (I use a prepared pack)

### TO MAKE AHEAD

This recipe can be stored cooked (without the pomegranate seed garnish), in the fridge for up to 3 days or freezer for 3 months. If using from frozen, defrost in the fridge. Heat through thoroughly on the hob or in the microwave.

# SIDE
# CAULIFLOWER CHEESE

**V**

**45 MINS**

This was never a side dish at Christmas when I was growing up, but somehow, it's ended up as a non-negotiable for so many of us as part of the festive feast. I mean, I'd happily eat this for breakfast, lunch and dinner any day of the year, so it's no surprise really is it? This recipe includes a white sauce shortcut as, over the years, so many of you have told me that you have found sauce-making intimidating. I hope I've made this easy enough so that even a non-cook can welcome the joy of cauliflower cheese into their life.

1. Preheat the oven to 200°C fan/220°C/Gas Mark 7.

2. Cook the cauliflower in a large saucepan of boiling salted water for 5–7 minutes, until the florets are almost, but not quite, cooked. (When you poke a knife into a stem it should be just tender.)

3. While the cauliflower is cooking, start making the cheese sauce. Measure the milk in a measuring jug. In a small bowl mix the cornflour with a splash of the milk from the jug. Use just enough to whisk the cornflour to a thick, lump-free paste (this feels a bit tricky, but it will come together eventually).

4. Pour the remaining milk into a small saucepan and place over a medium heat. Add the cornflour paste, whisk in, and cook for 5–10 minutes until the sauce starts to thicken, whisking often. Add the mustard, garlic granules, plenty of salt and pepper and the grated cheeses. Whisk and cook for another 5 minutes until the cheese is melted and the sauce is thick and smooth.

5. Drain the cauliflower well (make sure it's as dry as possible) and place in an ovenproof dish. Pour over the sauce and sprinkle the extra cheeses on top.

6. Bake in the preheated oven for 15–20 minutes until the cheese on top is melting and golden.

## SERVES 6 (AS A SIDE DISH)

**700g** cauliflower (a medium cauliflower), cut into florets
**500ml** milk (whole or semi-skimmed)
**30g** cornflour
**1 tsp** Dijon mustard
**1 tsp** garlic granules
**100g** Red Leicester cheese, grated
**75g** Parmesan cheese, grated
sea salt and freshly ground black pepper

### For the Topping
**25g** Red Leicester cheese, grated
**25g** Parmesan cheese, grated

### TO MAKE AHEAD
Prepare up to the end of step 4. Cover and store in the fridge for up to 48 hours until you're ready to cook. Finish in the oven as per step 5, allowing an extra 10–15 minutes' cooking time (because it will be very cold from the fridge). Ensure the centre is piping hot before serving.

If serving to vegetarians, use a suitable Parmesan alternative.

CAULIFLOWER
CHEESE

BRAISED RED
CABBAGE
*p.61*

# YORKSHIRE PUDDINGS

**50 MINS**

Whether or not Yorkshire Puddings have any place on a plate of roast turkey is often a point for hot debate. If you are that way inclined, this recipe has handy advice on how to make them in advance and reheat them on the day. I'd definitely advise that method as it's vital to successful Yorkshires that the oven door doesn't get opened during their first cook – tricky on Christmas Day!

1. **To make the batter, whisk the flour and salt with the eggs until you have a smooth, thick paste. Add about a third of the milk, whisk until smooth, then add the rest of the milk, along with the water and whisk again until totally smooth. Transfer your batter into a large jug if you have one (this will help you to safely pour later). For best results, if you have time, pop into the fridge to rest for 15–30 minutes (you can leave it for longer in the fridge if it's helpful to your timings, but you'll need to give it a very good stir and may need to add a little more milk to return it to its original consistency).**

2. **Preheat the oven to 220°C fan/240°C/Gas Mark 9.**

3. **When you're ready to cook, pour a little of the oil into each of the muffin tin holes and put into the oven for 10 minutes until the oil is smoking hot. Very carefully, open the oven door and remove the tray of hot oil (close the oven door swiftly). Working very quickly, pour or spoon the batter into each muffin hole (it should be hissing and bubbling). Return to the oven and reduce the oven temperature to 200°C fan/220°C/Gas Mark 7.**

4. **Cook for 30 minutes, until they are a deep dark golden colour and very crispy. DO NOT OPEN THE OVEN until at least 25 minutes has passed! Place the tray as close to the top of the oven as possible, but not so close that the puddings will touch the oven roof. Remove from the oven and serve.**

## MAKES 12 PUDDINGS

**150g** plain flour
pinch of salt
**3** eggs
**200ml** milk
  (whole or semi-skimmed)
**50ml** water
**2 tbsp** sunflower oil

**You will need:** 12-hole muffin tin

## TO MAKE AHEAD

Bake as per step 4, but cook for 25 minutes only. Remove from the oven and allow to cool fully. Store in the fridge for 3 days or the freezer for 3 months. Defrost, then heat in the oven (at 200°C fan/220°C/ Gas Mark 7) loose on a baking tray for 5–10 minutes from the fridge, or 10–15 minutes from frozen, until crisp and golden.

# SIDE
# SAUSAGE & APRICOT STUFFING

**1 HOUR**

Growing up in the 80s, the stuffing most often known to me came from a box. This is something entirely different. With intensely savoury meat and juicy chunks of apricot, it's divine with a roast and equally good (perhaps even better?) sliced cold in a sandwich the next day. I have to say I've never bothered with stuffing the turkey itself, as I very much like the crunchy edges this stuffing gets as it cooks in its own dish.

1. Preheat the oven to 180°C fan/200°C/Gas Mark 6.

2. Put the butter and onion in a small frying pan over a medium heat and cook for 5–10 minutes until slightly softened but not coloured.

3. Remove the skins of the sausages – cutting along the long edge of each sausage and then turning them inside out – and discard the skins. Put the sausage meat in a large bowl with the cooked onion (and the butter it cooked in) and all the remaining ingredients. Stir until thoroughly mixed (you may need to use clean hands!).

4. Spoon the mixture into a shallow ovenproof dish (don't smooth the top, as the lumps and bumps give a good texture).

5. Bake in the oven for 45 minutes, until cooked through and golden on top.

## SERVES 6

**25g** unsalted butter
**1** onion, peeled and finely chopped
**450g** pork sausages (or 8 sausages)
**50g** dried apricots, quartered
**90g** cooked chestnuts (the vacuum-packed type), roughly chopped
**50g** breadcrumbs (such as panko)
**10g** fresh sage leaves, finely chopped
sea salt

## TO MAKE AHEAD

Follow the recipe to step 4. Cover and put it in the fridge for up to 48 hours. When you're ready, cook as per step 5, but be aware it may take an extra 5–10 minutes in the oven if it's come straight out of the fridge.

Alternatively, make the recipe to step 4, cover and freeze for up to 1 month. Allow it to defrost fully before baking as from step 5.

# SAGE & ONION STUFFING BALLS

**55 MINS**

This vegetarian (and vegan) recipe is a definite upgrade from those boxes of just-add-water stuffing mix, but it's almost as simple to make. I use dry ready-made panko breadcrumbs for this as they are so easy to keep stocked in the cupboard and far less faff than making your own, especially at this time of year.

1. **Heat the butter or plant-based alternative and olive oil in a large frying pan over a low-medium heat, add the onion and cook for 10 minutes or until softened but not coloured (turn the heat down if they are starting to brown). Add the garlic, sage and pepper and cook for a further 5 minutes until the garlic is softened, then remove from the heat and stir in the breadcrumbs and stock. Mix well, cover and leave to stand for 10 minutes.**

2. **Using clean hands, take a small ball of stuffing and check that it will stick together into a ball. (If it won't, add a tablespoon or two of boiling water, stir in well and check again until it will – this will depend on the type of breadcrumbs you use, so you need to test it as you go!)**

3. **When the stuffing is the right consistency, add a little olive oil to the palm of your hand and roll the stuffing into 12 balls. You will need to press and squeeze them quite firmly. If you're not cooking them immediately, chill them in the fridge until you are ready to bake them. If you have time to chill them for an hour or more, they will tend to keep their shape better when baked.**

4. **Preheat the oven to 200°C fan/220°C/Gas Mark 7. Put the balls into a small baking dish and bake for 25–35 minutes or until crispy and golden.**

### MAKES 12 BALLS

**50g** salted butter
(or plant-based alternative)
**1 tbsp** olive oil, plus extra for rolling
**1** onion, peeled and finely chopped
**2** garlic cloves, peeled and crushed
**5g** fresh sage, finely chopped
**¼ tsp** freshly ground black pepper
**125g** breadcrumbs (such as panko)
**200ml** hot vegetable stock
(made from a cube is fine)

### TO MAKE AHEAD

Make up to step 3. Store in the fridge for up to 24 hours before baking as per step 4.

# MAKE-AHEAD GRAVY

**VG**

## 2 HOURS 20 MINS

If there's just one recipe you make in advance, let it be this one. Making gravy on the big day, using the bottom of the roasting tin after your meat is cooked is, of course, delicious, but – oh my goodness – the pressure that adds to the whole proceedings is something else. The added benefit of using this method is that the gravy is accidentally vegan (if you use suitable wine), so everyone can enjoy it. It does take a while to let this roast and bubble for maximum flavour, so I often cook a double batch and freeze it in portions for anytime a meal calls for gravy.

1. **Preheat the oven to 200°C fan/220°C/Gas Mark 7.**

2. **Start by preparing the vegetables, cut the tops and bottom off each onion, remove the outermost later of skin, but leave on as much of the rest of the skin as you can, then cut in half, and each half into quarters. Cut the leeks, carrots and celery into 2cm chunks (you can leave the carrots unpeeled). Cut the top off the garlic bulb.**

3. **Put all the vegetables on a baking tray, drizzle with the olive oil, and add a good seasoning of salt and pepper. Put in the oven and set a timer for 50 minutes.**

4. **When the timer goes off, remove the tray from the oven, give everything a good shake and add the tomato purée and thyme. Return to the oven for 10 minutes, until the vegetables have turned very brown, then transfer them to a large saucepan. Carefully squeeze the garlic out of its skin into the vegetables, add the bay leaves, stock cubes, water and white wine, bring to the boil, then reduce the heat and simmer for 1 hour (it should be bubbling).**

5. **Using a large sieve, strain the mixture into a large bowl, discarding the vegetables. Pour the gravy back into the saucepan.**

6. **Put the cornflour in a small dish and add just enough of the gravy to make a smooth paste (making this cornflour paste helps avoid lumps). Pour the paste back into the saucepan of gravy and mix well. Add the soy sauce and redcurrant jelly and cook over a low heat for a further 5–10 minutes until thickened, whisking often to avoid any lumps.**

### SERVES 6

**2** onions
**500g** leeks
**450g** carrots
**4** celery sticks
**1** garlic bulb
**2 tbsp** olive oil
**2 tbsp** tomato purée
**10g** fresh thyme
**2** bay leaves
**2** vegetable stock cubes
  (no need to dilute)
**1.5 litres** water
**180ml** white wine (check the label
  if you're vegetarian or vegan)
**25g** cornflour
**2 tbsp** dark soy sauce
  (I use reduced salt)
**2 tbsp** redcurrant jelly
sea salt and freshly ground
  black pepper

### TO MAKE AHEAD

When the gravy is cold pour it into a freezer-safe container and freeze for up to 3 months. Freeze in one batch or separate into a couple. Defrost thoroughly in the fridge overnight and reheat over a medium heat in a saucepan on the hob until hot through.

Replace the wine with additional water if you prefer an alcohol free version.

CRANBERRY
SAUCE
*p.72*

MAKE-AHEAD GRAVY

BREAD SAUCE
*p.73*

# CRANBERRY SAUCE

**25 MINS, PLUS COOLING TIME**

This classic accompaniment to turkey is so much better than shop-bought cranberry sauce in a jar. I'm all for making life simpler, but this is so much tastier and it's incredibly easy to make. Leftovers keep well in the fridge and are perfect for turkey sandwiches. I like my cranberry sauce quite tart, so if you like a sweeter sauce you may want to add some more sugar.

1. **Put the orange juice, zest and sugar in a saucepan over a medium heat and warm through until the sugar has completely dissolved. Add the cranberries and bring to the boil, reduce the heat and simmer for about 15 minutes until the cranberry skins have burst and the sauce has begun to thicken.**

2. **Remove from the heat and leave to thicken as it cools – this should take about 15 minutes.**

---

**SERVES 6–8**

**1** orange, zested and juiced
(you need about 75ml juice)
**75g** caster sugar
**200g** cranberries, fresh or frozen

---

**TO MAKE AHEAD**

You can make up to 1 week ahead: refrigerate in an airtight container.

# BREAD SAUCE

**15 MINUTES, PLUS COOLING TIME**

Every Christmas, I say I'm not going to bother making bread sauce and every year I do make it because I can't help but succumb to a spoonful or two of it. It's out of fashion now perhaps, but I couldn't write a Christmas recipe book and not include it as this creamy, comforting, lightly spiced sauce is such a classic. You can freeze leftovers to serve with roast chicken at a later date.

1. **Heat the milk with the onion, bay leaves and peppercorns in a small saucepan over a medium heat. Allow it to come to the boil, so that the surface is bubbling, then turn off the heat and set aside for 30 minutes.**

2. **Pour the milk into a jug through a sieve, removing the onion, bay leaves and peppercorns (discard these). Return the milk to the pan over a low heat. Add the breadcrumbs and plenty of salt and pepper. Keep the heat low and stir continuously for 3–5 minutes or until the sauce is very thick.**

3. **Add the double cream and stir over the low heat for about 1–2 minutes until hot through (add more double cream if you like, depending on how thick you like your bread sauce). Season to taste with salt and pepper.**

---

### SERVES 6–8

**400ml** milk
  (whole or semi-skimmed)
**1** onion, peeled and quartered
**3** bay leaves
about **15** whole black peppercorns
**75g** breadcrumbs (such as panko)
**4–6 tbsp** double cream
sea salt and freshly ground
  black pepper

---

### TO MAKE AHEAD

You can make up to 3 days in advance (keeping it in the fridge, covered) and reheat it in microwave or hob. It will thicken further if you do this. Add a little more milk and/or cream to get the texture you'd like.

# Nibbles

All of the recipes in this chapter can be served as part of a buffet, as snacks for visitors, or before your Christmas Day meal.

In recent years I've tended to serve 2 or 3 different nibbles before the main meal rather than a starter. I'm a fan of this approach as it avoids another round of washing up!

It's also a more relaxed way to eat while opening presents and enjoying the general chaos of the day.

All of these dishes are designed to be particularly quick and simple so you can focus on the main Christmas lunch (in preparation and appetite!).

# PRAWN COCKTAIL CUPS

**15 MINS**

Prawn cocktail has been a go-to Christmas starter since the 1970s and quite rightly so, it's a classic. Serving it like this, in lettuce leaves, just means that people can eat as many or as few as they like, they can be served as part of a buffet and, dare I say, they also look a little more stylish than the original (I think).

1. **Cut away the base of the lettuces and carefully separate the leaves. Wash and dry the leaves.**

2. **Mix the prawns with the mayonnaise, ketchup and Worcestershire sauce (or Henderson's relish) in a small bowl.**

3. **Spoon the filling into the lettuce leaves just before serving and sprinkle with a little paprika and a few chopped chives.**

### SERVES 6 (AS A NIBBLE)

**2** little gem lettuces
**300g** cooked and peeled prawns
**100g** mayonnaise
**2 tbsp** tomato ketchup
**1 tsp** Worcestershire sauce
   (or Henderson's relish)

**To Serve**
pinch of paprika
fresh chives, finely chopped

### TO MAKE AHEAD

Prepare the lettuce and the prawns in sauce and store, covered, in the fridge for up to 24 hours, until you're ready to serve. Fill the lettuce cups just before serving.

Use fresh, cooked prawns or frozen, defrosted, cooked prawns.

# SMOKED SALMON CANAPÉS

**20 MINS**

Always a favourite canapé, a tray of these appearing at Christmas can't help but feel luxurious. I use a speedy little dressing which adds extra flavour. If you're not a fan of horseradish, replace it with a little lemon juice instead.

1. **Mix the crème fraîche with the horseradish sauce in a small bowl and set aside.**

2. **Butter the bread and cut off the crusts. Cut each slice into quarters.**

3. **Cut the salmon into small strips and sit a bite-sized piece on top of each of the squares of buttered bread.**

4. **When you're ready to serve, spoon a little of the sauce on top of each piece of salmon and top with fresh dill and black pepper.**

### SERVES 6 (AS A NIBBLE)

**200g** crème fraîche
**1½ tsp** horseradish sauce
**6** slices of wholemeal/granary bread, from an 800g loaf
**75g** salted butter, at room temperature
**150g** sliced smoked salmon

**To Serve**
fresh dill, chopped
freshly ground black pepper

### TO MAKE AHEAD

Butter and top the bread with the salmon up to 2 hours before serving. Make the sauce and store both separately in the fridge. Top with the sauce and garnishes just before serving.

# BAKED CAMEMBERT

**20 MINS**

I would like to point out here that the number of servings is very much a guide. I would happily sit and eat a whole baked camembert alone – just me?! Last year I spent many joyful hours testing the perfect method for baking camembert, and here it is. Serve with crackers, breadsticks, crudités or charcuterie to dunk. This recipe works equally well with a whole wheel of brie.

1. **Preheat the oven to 180°C fan/200°C/Gas Mark 6.**

2. **Open the camembert box and peel away the paper wrapper that the cheese is stored in. Return the cheese to the base of the box (if it doesn't have a box, see notes!). Using a sharp knife, score the top of the cheese and poke the garlic slices into the cuts. Drizzle over the honey and sprinkle with the thyme and salt.**

3. **Sit the box on a baking tray and bake in the oven for 15–18 minutes, or until the cheese is turning golden on top and is very soft within.**

4. **Serve immediately.**

## SERVES 4–6 (AS A NIBBLE)

**1** whole camembert, about 250g
**2** garlic cloves, peeled and thinly sliced
**1 tbsp** runny honey
**2 tsp** fresh thyme leaves
**½ tsp** sea salt

## TO MAKE AHEAD

Prepare your camembert and keep it in the fridge, uncooked, for up to 24 hours until just before you're ready to bake.

If your camembert doesn't have a box, remove any packaging, wrap it in a layer of baking paper or foil to make a parcel, sit it onto a baking tray and bake.

# GOAT'S CHEESE BITES

**10 MINS**

This is my go-to nibble to make when I have very limited time but want to impress. Each bite is the perfect creamy cheese combo. They work particularly well with those fancy crackers sold in delis, with fruit and nuts in them. Otherwise, any small bite-sized savoury biscuit is fine.

1. **Cut the goat's cheese into 18 small pieces.**

2. **Spread the crackers with chutney, add the goat's cheese and sprinkle each one with chopped walnuts.**

### SERVES 6 (AS A NIBBLE)

**75g** soft goat's cheese
(the type that is sold in a log)
**100g** chutney (or your own
homemade chutney – page 178)
**18** small crackers
**18** walnuts (about 40g),
roughly chopped

### TO MAKE AHEAD

You can make this nibble up
to 2 hours ahead of serving.
Store in the fridge.

If serving to vegetarians, check
that the cheese is suitable.

# SMASHED PEA CROSTINI

**15 MINS**

We've all heard of avocado on toast, but have you heard of peas on toast?! This vibrant green topping is very handy to make with peas from the freezer (no waiting for avocado to ripen!). If you don't need these to be vegan, top with some shaved Parmesan or crumbled feta.

1. **Put the peas in a large heatproof bowl, pour over enough boiling water to cover and leave for 5–10 minutes until defrosted.**

2. **Grate the zest of one of the lemons into a small dish and set aside (for garnishing).**

3. **Drain the peas and add them to your food processor or mini chopper along with the mint, cashew nuts, olive oil and plenty of salt and pepper. Add the grated zest of the second lemon, along with the juice of both lemons (avoid the pips!). Blend until it forms a chunky paste – you may need to scrape down the sides of the chopper/ food processor as you go.**

4. **Lightly toast the bread slices on both sides.**

5. **Spread a dollop of the pea purée on each piece of bread and top with reserved lemon zest.**

---

### SERVES 6 (AS A NIBBLE)

**150g** frozen peas
**2** lemons
**10g** fresh mint
**100g** unsalted cashew nuts
**4 tbsp** olive oil
(extra virgin if you have it)
French bread or sourdough baguette,
cut into about 18 x 5mm-thick slices
sea salt and freshly ground
black pepper

**You will need:** food processor or mini chopper

---

### TO MAKE AHEAD

Up to 24 hours before serving, toast the bread and store in an airtight container. Make the topping, cover and store in the fridge. Assemble just before serving.

---

If serving to vegans, check that the bread is suitable.

**SMASHED PEA CROSTINI**
*p.83*

**PARMA HAM & MELON BITES**
*p.86*

**BRIE & CRANBERRY BITES**
*p.87*

**GOAT'S CHEESE BITES**
*p.82*

# PARMA HAM & MELON BITES

**20 MINS**

Serving melon as a starter might seem quite dated, but it's worth reviving that 1970s trend for these small bites. Juicy melon, wrapped in salty Italian ham, they are the perfect fresh treat, especially before a rich meal.

1. **Cut the melon in half, remove the seeds and peel.**

2. **Cut each melon half into 3cm-thick slices, then cut each slice into bite-sized chunks.**

3. **Halve each slice of Parma ham and wrap a piece around each melon chunk.**

4. **Just before serving, drizzle the melon and ham with the olive oil and add a sprinkling of shredded mint.**

### SERVES 6 (AS A NIBBLE)

**1** ripe cantaloupe melon (or half if your melon is very large)
**160g** Parma ham
**2 tsp** olive oil
(extra virgin if you have it)
**5g** fresh mint leaves, finely shredded

### TO MAKE AHEAD

Cut up your melon, wrap in Parma ham, and store in an airtight container in the fridge for up to 24 hours. Just before serving, arrange on a plate and drizzle with olive oil and sprinkle over the mint.

# BRIE & CRANBERRY BITES

**40 MINS**

Two of the best food groups (pastry and cheese) in one bite. You could replace the cranberry sauce with any chutney if you prefer. This recipe is also a brilliant way of using up leftover cheese after Christmas – perfect for a new year celebration, or a treat to brighten up January.

1. Preheat the oven to 200°C fan/220°C/Gas Mark 7 and brush the inside of the 12 holes of the muffin tin with the olive oil.

2. Unroll the puff pastry sheet, cut it into 12 squares and push into each muffin hole. Spoon a little of the cranberry sauce into each pastry square, then sit a piece of brie on top. Brush the pastry with beaten egg.

3. Bake in the oven for 20–25 minutes or until crisp and golden.

4. Remove from the oven, sprinkle with salt and drizzle with honey to serve.

## SERVES 6 (AS A NIBBLE)

**320g** ready-rolled puff pastry sheet
**100g** cranberry sauce (shop-bought or see page 72)
**150g** brie, cut into 12 pieces
**1** egg, beaten
olive oil, for greasing

**To Serve**
sea salt
runny honey

**You will need:** 12-hole muffin tin

## TO MAKE AHEAD

Keep in the fridge uncooked, and covered, for up to 3 days. Remove from the fridge and bake.

★

If serving to vegetarians, check that the cheese is suitable.

# HONEY MUSTARD SAUSAGES

**30 MINS**

If there is one Christmas recipe I cook that has everyone flocking to the kitchen, it is these. They are almost impossible not to nibble on straight from the oven – be careful though, the honey gets very hot!

1. Preheat the oven to 180°C fan/200°C/Gas Mark 6.

2. Tip the sausages onto a baking tray, drizzle over the oil and toss them to lightly coat.

3. Bake in the oven for 20–25 minutes or until browned and cooked through.

4. Remove from the oven and if there is lots of fat on the baking tray drain this away.

5. Pour over the honey and wholegrain mustard and give everything a good stir so the sausages are well coated. Return to the oven for 5 minutes until sticky. Stir well and serve with any remaining drizzle from the tray poured over.

### SERVES 6 (AS A NIBBLE)

**300g** uncooked cocktail sausages (about 18)
**1 tsp** sunflower oil
**2 tbsp** runny honey
**1 tbsp** wholegrain mustard

### TO MAKE AHEAD

Part-bake the sausages for about 15–20 minutes until just starting to turn brown. Allow to cool. Cover and keep in the fridge for up to 24 hours until you are ready to serve. Now add the honey and mustard and put in a preheated oven for 10–15 minutes until cooked through, sticky and golden.

# Festive Breakfasts

All of the recipes in this chapter are designed to be suitable to serve on Christmas morning without distracting you too much from the excitement of the festivities.

They can be made ahead, or partly prepared ahead.

I generally try to keep breakfast on Christmas morning fairly light, ready for the main event later.

# CHRISTMAS MORNING MUFFINS

**30 MINS, PLUS COOLING TIME**

The smell of baking in the morning is always a treat, especially on Christmas Day. These spiced muffins are ready in less than half an hour from start to finish, but when I am trying to keep all kitchen faffing to a minimum on the big day, I like to bake them the day before. Reheat them slightly in the oven the next day before serving for breakfast.

1. Preheat the oven to 180°C fan/200°C/Gas Mark 6 and line a muffin tin with 12 muffin cases.

2. Put all the wet ingredients in a jug and whisk until fully combined.

3. In a separate bowl, combine the dry ingredients.

4. Add the wet ingredients to the dry ingredients and mix until you have a smooth batter, with no visible lumps of flour. Spoon the mixture evenly among the muffin cases and bake in the oven for 15–17 minutes until golden on top and springy to the touch.

5. Remove from the oven, carefully take the muffins from the tin and leave to cool on a wire rack.

## MAKES 12 MUFFINS

**Wet Ingredients**
**175ml** whole milk
**100ml** sunflower oil
**75g** runny honey
**1** egg

**Dry Ingredients**
**200g** plain flour
**50g** rolled oats
**2½ tsp** baking powder
**½ tsp** bicarbonate of soda
**1 tsp** mixed spice
**1** orange, zested
**150g** dried cranberries

**You will need:** 12-hole muffin tin and 12 muffin cases

### TO MAKE AHEAD

Bake as per the recipe, cool and store in an airtight container for up to 3 days. Before serving, warm in a preheated oven at 200°C fan/220°C/Gas Mark 7 for 8–10 minutes. These can also be frozen for up to 3 months. Defrost at room temperature before reheating in the oven.

# CROISSANT CHRISTMAS TREE

**45 MINS**

Pull-apart pastry Christmas trees are all over the internet, but I like to make mine a little differently, using ready-made croissant dough. You can swap in sheets of puff pastry if you can't find cans of uncooked croissant dough, but this works so well for breakfast if you can use it. A little nifty cutting and rolling and there's no waste either.

1. Preheat the oven to 200°C fan/220°C/Gas Mark 7 and line a baking tray with baking paper.

2. Carefully open the tin of dough and unroll it. Place it on the lined baking tray. Cut the long strip in half and lay each half side by side so it forms a wider rectangle. Squish the join so they become one piece. Cut a line from the middle of the top edge, to the bottom left corner, and another line from the middle of the top edge to the bottom right corner. (You want one big triangle and two smaller ones either side.) Cover the middle large triangle with the chocolate spread and spread it evenly.

3. Take the two smaller triangles you cut and flip them over so that you can sit them on top of the chocolate spread to join up and make a large triangle for the top. Squish the join in the middle, or any other gaps, together with your fingers.

4. Cut strips either side using scissors, about 3cm wide. Don't cut all the way to the middle. Trim off any messy or uneven bits at the bottom (save this). Twist each of the side strips two or three times.

5. Use any offcut dough to cut out a small star to top the tree. Brush with beaten egg and bake in the oven for 20–25 minutes until golden all over.

**SERVES 6**

**340g** ready-made croissant dough (the type in a tin)
**250g** chocolate spread
**1** egg, beaten

**TO MAKE AHEAD**

Prepare this the night before, cover and store in the fridge ready for baking.

CROISSANT
CHRISTMAS
TREE
*p.94*

CHRISTMAS
GRANOLA
*p.98*

CHRISTMAS
MORNING MUFFINS
*p.92*

# CHRISTMAS GRANOLA

**40 MINS, PLUS COOLING TIME**

This can be made well ahead of the big day (up to 2 weeks in fact) and stored in an airtight container. Serve it on Christmas morning with a dish of Greek yoghurt and some fresh berries (or your Christmas Tree Fruit Salad on page 100) for everyone to help themselves. Small bags of this would also work brilliantly as homemade gifts, tied with some ribbon.

1. Preheat the oven to 160°C fan/180°C/Gas Mark 4 and line a baking tray with baking paper (if yours isn't non-stick).

2. Whisk the egg white in a very clean bowl until light and fluffy, but not stiff (use a hand-held electric whisk if you have one). Mix in all of the other ingredients (except the cranberries) until well coated.

3. Tip the mix onto the baking tray and bake in the oven for 15 minutes, remove from the oven and gently stir, then bake for a further 10–15 minutes until golden.

4. Remove from the oven, mix in the cranberries, then leave to cool and harden before serving (or storing in an airtight container).

## TO MAKE WITH A SLOW COOKER

Follow step 2 above, add all of the ingredients (except the cranberries) to your slow cooker and cook on HIGH with the lid on but slightly ajar. It will take 1½– 2½ hours to cook: after 1 hour, stir gently to check it is not sticking. Stop it cooking when it's just starting to get crunchy (it won't be fully crunchy, only around the edges, the rest will 'crunch' as it cools). Tip it out onto a baking tray, stir in the cranberries and leave to cool.

### SERVES 6–8

**2** egg whites
**250g** jumbo oats
**6 tbsp** runny honey
**2 tsp** mixed spice
**2** oranges, zested
**150g** pecan nuts, roughly chopped
**100g** dried cranberries, to finish

### TO MAKE AHEAD

Store in an airtight container for up to 2 weeks.

★

This recipe uses only the egg whites; you could use the leftover yolks for the trifle custard on page 156.

# CHRISTMAS TREE FRUIT SALAD

**15 MINS**

Sometimes the simplest ideas are the most effective and this is one of them. Every year my children go wild over this fruit salad. To keep the festive theme, stick to red and green fruits. Apples work well too but toss them in a little lemon juice first to stop them browning.

1. **Wash the grapes, raspberries and strawberries. If you're serving to young children, cut the grapes into small pieces.**

2. **Using a plate, tray or board, arrange each type of fruit in a row to make a Christmas-tree shape (I like to use a tray covered with greaseproof paper, or a large wooden cutting board).**

### SERVES 6

**375g** grapes
**150g** raspberries
**225g** strawberries, hulled and halved
**100g** kiwis, peeled and cut into 1cm-thick slices

### TO MAKE AHEAD

Peel and chop the fruit the night before, cover and store in the fridge overnight.

# HASH BROWN BREAKFAST BAKE

**45 MINS**

This breakfast bake feels like something you might find in a retro American diner. I love a potato-based breakfast and here I've used frozen hash browns as a nifty shortcut to peeling and grating your own. It's a brilliant recipe to prep in advance.

1. **Preheat the oven to 180°C fan/200°C/Gas Mark 6.**

2. **Put a small frying pan over a high heat and add the bacon lardons (you shouldn't need any oil as they usually have plenty of fat – if yours don't, add 1 teaspoon sunflower oil to the pan). Cook for 5–10 minutes until brown all over.**

3. **Beat the eggs in a small bowl, add the cooked bacon and grated cheese and mix to combine.**

4. **Arrange the frozen hash browns in a shallow baking dish (about 27 x 20cm) and scatter over the halved tomatoes. Pour the egg mixture over the top and sprinkle with the spring onions.**

5. **Bake in the oven for 25–30 minutes until the eggs are set in the middle. Serve.**

### SERVES 4

**180g** smoked bacon lardons
**8** eggs
**75g** mature Cheddar cheese, grated
**625g** shop-bought frozen
hash browns
**250g** cherry tomatoes, halved
**4** spring onions, trimmed and
finely chopped

### TO MAKE AHEAD

Prepare this the night before, up to the end of step 4, and store in the fridge uncooked, ready to pop into the oven on Christmas morning. It may take 5–10 minutes longer to cook if it's very cold from the fridge.

To make this vegetarian
leave out the bacon.

# CHRISTMAS MORNING COCKTAIL CUBES

**OVERNIGHT**

These ice cubes are an impressive alternative to the usual Christmas morning Buck's Fizz. They are simple but so effective when you pop them into a glass on Christmas morning. Pour over sparkling wine (or a non-alcoholic alternative) and as the ice cubes melt, your juice cocktail appears.

1.  **Put an orange wedge and some cranberries (the amount will depend on how big your ice cube tray is) into each section of the ice cube tray. Add a small sprig of rosemary to each, poking out from the top a little, and fill the remainder of each cube with orange juice. Repeat until all sections are full. Freeze overnight.**

2.  **When ready to serve, pop one or two in a champagne glass and top up with prosecco (or a non-alcoholic alternative).**

**SERVES ABOUT 6**

**1** or **2** oranges, cut into small wedges
fresh cranberries
fresh rosemary
orange juice
Prosecco/champagne (check the label if you are vegetarian or vegan) or non-alcoholic alternative, to serve

**You will need:** ice cube tray (I use a large silicone one)

**TO MAKE AHEAD**

Store the ice cubes in the freezer for up to 1 month.

# Cooking for a Crowd

At this time of year, we can often find ourselves catering
to a larger group of people in one sitting,
not just the for the big day, but celebrations around that.

This chapter has ideas for easy hands-off recipes
that are all-round crowd pleasers.

Mix and match to make your perfect menu.

# SLOW COOKER
# ROASTED GAMMON

**6 HOURS**

There is something particularly festive about serving golden, glistening roasted gammon as a centrepiece for a buffet table. My family tradition is to start this off on the morning of Christmas Eve, then serve it with baked potatoes and salads in the evening, going on to nibble on the leftovers at every possible opportunity between Christmas and New Year. Leftover meat can also be frozen – it makes a happy discovery to perk up pies or pastas in January.

1.  **Put the slow cook ingredients into the slow cooker. Place the lid on and cook on HIGH for 4–6 hours or LOW for 6–8 hours. If you can, turn the joint over and baste it halfway through the cooking time.**

2.  **When the cooking time is complete, take the meat out of the slow cooker and discard the vegetables and liquid.**

3.  **Preheat the oven to 200°C fan/220°C/Gas Mark 7 and line a roasting tin with two layers of tin foil or use a disposable tin-foil tray. (This is important, as the glaze is incredibly hard to scrub off!)**

4.  **Remove the string and layer of skin (if your gammon has them) and use a sharp knife to score the fat. Sit the ham in the lined pan and drench it with the honey. Pat the sugar (and mustard powder if you're using it) onto the honey. Roast for 30 minutes until the ham is just turning black at the edges.**

## TO MAKE WITHOUT A SLOW COOKER

Work out the cooking time of your gammon joint by calculating 30 minutes per 450g/1lb, plus an additional 30 minutes. Put the 'slow cook' ingredients into a large saucepan and boil on the hob over a medium heat for the total cooking time minus 30 minutes. Drain, add the honey and sugar and finish in the oven as per steps 3 and 4 above.

### SERVES 6–8 (AS PART OF A BUFFET)

**For the Slow Cook**
**1** gammon joint (boneless, smoked or unsmoked), about 2kg
**1** carrot, peeled and quartered
**1** onion, peeled and quartered
**3 tbsp** mixed spice
**500ml** cider (dry or medium)
**1 litre** apple juice

**For the Glaze**
**6 tbsp** runny honey
**3 tbsp** soft dark brown sugar
**1 tbsp** English mustard powder (optional)

### TO MAKE AHEAD

Allow the baked ham to cool, wrap well and store in the fridge for up to 3 days, until ready to slice and serve cold.

If you prefer not to cook with alcohol, replace the cider with additional apple juice.

# FESTIVE BRAISED BEEF

**3 HOURS 30 MINS**

I'm all about recipes being as simple as possible, though if I'm cooking for a crowd and can peacefully make something well in advance, I don't mind a little initial faffing as it's all done and dusted by the time guests arrive, when I should be having fun. Case in point: peeling shallots. I can't usually muster any enthusiasm for such a task but at this time of year, when I want to impress and if, and only if, it can be done in advance, I'm happy to make time to elevate this above my usual beef stew, and I hope you are too. (Also, top tip: soak shallots in boiling water for 5 minutes and they are then a doddle to peel!)

1. **Preheat the oven to 160°C fan/180°C/Gas Mark 4.**

2. **Heat 1 tablespoon of the olive oil in your largest saucepan over a high heat. Pat the diced beef dry with kitchen paper, then add some of it to the pan (don't overcrowd the pan). Cook for 5–10 minutes, turning the pieces occasionally, until they are turning golden brown all over. Transfer to a bowl, set aside, and repeat with the rest of the oil and diced beef until it is all browned, then remove from the pan.**

3. **Put the pan back on the hob, add the pancetta or bacon and cook over a high heat for 5–10 minutes until crisp all over. Add the shallots and carrots, stir well and cook for a further 10 minutes until they have begun to soften. Sprinkle over the flour and stir everything well so it's coated (this may be tricky depending on the size of your pan, but you'll get there, I have faith in you). Add the tomato purée, mixed spice, red wine and beef stock. Give it all a good stir, put the lid on and cook in the oven for 3–3½ hours or until the beef is very tender (stir it occasionally if you're passing the oven).**

4. **Before serving, mix in the cranberry sauce.**

## TO MAKE WITH A SLOW COOKER

Reduce the stock quantity to 200ml. Add all of the ingredients (except the cranberry sauce) to your slow cooker, pop the lid on and cook on HIGH for 5–6 hours or LOW for 7–9 hours. Add your cranberry sauce to finish, as above.

### SERVES 8–10 (AS PART OF A BUFFET)

**2 tbsp** olive oil
**1.5kg** diced beef
**260g** diced pancetta (or smoked bacon lardons)
**450g** shallots, peeled and trimmed
**450g** carrots, peeled and cut into 2cm chunks
**75g** plain flour
**3 tbsp** tomato purée
**1 tbsp** mixed spice
**375ml** red wine (or alcohol-free alternative)
**500ml** hot beef stock (made from a cube is fine)
sea salt and freshly ground black pepper

**To Finish**
**75g** cranberry sauce (shop-bought or see page 72)

### TO MAKE AHEAD

This recipe can be stored cooked, in the fridge for 3 days or freezer for 3 months. If frozen, defrost in the fridge. Heat thoroughly on the hob or in the microwave.

'Diced beef/cubed beef' is any kind of beef suitable for slow cooking, as sold in supermarkets. I find that they vary greatly in size, shape and tenderness so you may need to adjust the cooking time until the meat is tender.

## SLOW COOKER
# VEGETABLE & CASHEW CURRY

**5 HOURS 10 MINS**

Be sure to cut all of the vegetables quite small here. It gives the curry the best texture. I've kept this recipe at my usual serving size, assuming it will be served as a vegetarian option with other main courses, but if you have a large slow cooker (or if you're cooking on the hob) this can easily be doubled. It freezes very well too.

1. **Put all of the ingredients into the slow cooker (except the garam masala), pop the lid on and cook on HIGH for 5–6 hours or on LOW for 7–8 hours.**

2. **The curry is ready when the vegetables are softened but not broken down. Stir in the garam masala before serving.**

3. **Serve with rice, poppadums and mango chutney.**

## TO MAKE WITHOUT A SLOW COOKER

Cook all the ingredients (except the garam masala) in a saucepan on the hob over a medium heat for 30–40 minutes, softening the onion and garlic before adding the other ingredients. Stir in the garam masala before serving.

Use a curry paste to your own tastes and spice level (such as korma, or tikka masala). Check the packet for what is considered a serving for 4 people and adjust the amount in the recipe accordingly. It's usually 1–2 tablespoons per person but it may vary for different brands.

---

### SERVES 4–6 (AS PART OF A BUFFET)

**400g** cauliflower, cut into 1cm chunks
**500g** courgette, cut into 1cm cubes
**250g** aubergine, cut into 1cm cubes
**3** garlic cloves, peeled and crushed
**1** red onion, peeled and finely chopped
**4 tbsp** curry paste (see Note below)
**3 tbsp** tomato pureé
**1 x 400ml** tin coconut milk
**½ tsp** sea salt
**200g** unsalted cashew nuts
**1 tsp** garam masala

**To Serve**
cooked rice
poppadums
mango chutney

### TO MAKE AHEAD

This recipe is perfect for freezing as a 'dump bag', which is when you prepare raw ingredients for a slow cook and freeze them until you are ready to cook the meal. The curry can also be stored cooked, in the fridge for up to 3 days or freezer for up to 3 months. Defrost and heat through thoroughly on the hob or in the microwave.

# MOROCCAN-STYLE CHICKEN STEW

**4 HOURS 10 MINS**

This dish is something like a tagine, with warming spices to make it feel pleasingly festive. We're using the shortcut of ras el hanout, a ready-made spice blend, to save us mixing the 10 or more spices ourselves. You can find ras el hanout in most large supermarkets.

1. **Put all of the ingredients in a slow cooker pot (except the cornflour and stock).**

2. **Put the cornflour into a small dish and add just enough of the stock to make a smooth paste. Now add that paste back into the measuring jug of stock, mix well and add to the rest of the ingredients in the slow cooker. Add salt and pepper, pop the lid on and cook on HIGH for 3–4 hours or LOW for 6–8 hours, until the vegetables are softened, the sauce is thickened and the chicken falls apart easily.**

3. **Before serving, stir in the honey and sprinkle over the flaked almonds.**

## TO MAKE WITHOUT A SLOW COOKER

Cook everything in a lidded ovenproof dish in an oven preheated to 160°C fan/180°C/Gas Mark 4, or over a low heat, for 1 hour until the chicken is cooked through, the vegetables are soft and the sauce is thick. If the sauce becomes too thick, add an extra 100ml of water.

This method of mixing cornflour into a paste first is known as a 'slurry'. It is important as it is the only way to avoid lumpy cornflour!

### SERVES 6–8 (AS PART OF A BUFFET)

**1.2kg** skinless, boneless chicken thighs
**1** red onion, peeled and finely chopped
**1** aubergine, cut into 2cm cubes
**1 x 400g** tin chickpeas, drained and rinsed
**1 x 400g** tin chopped tomatoes
**2 tbsp** ras el hanout spice mix
**2 tsp** ground cumin
**100g** dried apricots, cut into small pieces
**2 tbsp** cornflour
**500ml** hot vegetable stock (made from a stock cube is fine)
sea salt and freshly ground black pepper

**To Serve**
**2 tbsp** runny honey
**30g** flaked almonds (toasted, if possible)

### TO MAKE AHEAD

This recipe is perfect for freezing as a 'dump bag' (prepare the raw ingredients for the slow cook and freeze until you are ready to cook the meal.) Freeze all the ingredients, minus the cornflour and stock. Add these per the recipe just before cooking. This recipe can also be stored cooked, in the fridge for 3 days or freezer for 3 months. If frozen, defrost in the fridge and heat thoroughly on the hob or in the microwave.

# CHEESE & TOMATO TART

**45 MINS**

The secret to this shortcut vegetarian centrepiece is mostly in displaying the tomatoes in an artful way. I try to buy a mixture of sizes and colours of tomato if I can find them, and then work around the pastry, overlapping them slightly. The end result is not only delicious, but really impressive to look at.

1.  Preheat the oven to 200°C fan/220°C/Gas Mark 7.

2.  Lay the pastry, together with the baking paper it comes with, out on a baking tray. Score a 5mm-wide border around the edge with a sharp knife.

3.  Mix together the cream cheese and pesto in a small bowl. Spread the pesto and cheese mixture evenly over the pastry sheet, within the 5mm border.

4.  Depending on the size of the tomatoes, either halve if cherry/small, or thinly slice if larger. Arrange them on top of the pesto and cream cheese mixture. Season well with salt and pepper and bake in the oven for 25–30 minutes until the pastry is golden.

5.  Remove from the oven, sprinkle over the basil and drizzle with olive oil before serving.

### SERVES 6–8 (AS PART OF A BUFFET)

**320g** ready-rolled puff pastry sheet
**200g** garlic and herb cream cheese
**2 tbsp** green pesto
**450g** tomatoes, a mixture
  of colours/sizes if you can
  find them
sea salt and freshly ground
  black pepper

**To Serve**
**10** fresh basil leaves, finely shredded
**1 tsp** olive oil

### TO MAKE AHEAD

Prepare the tart, cover and store in the fridge for up to 24 hours, uncooked. Bake just before you are ready to serve.

# ROASTED WINTER SALAD

**1 HOUR 10 MINS**

As an avid avoider of lettuce, this is far more enticing to me than most salads. It's also very helpful at this time of year that the ingredients can be bought well in advance – no last-minute supermarket dash for some greenery. If you're making the full recipe, you may need to spread it over two baking trays, so everything has space to cook. This can be eaten warm, or, if you're serving it from the fridge, allow it to come to room temperature.

1. **Preheat the oven to 200°C fan/220°C/Gas Mark 7.**

2. **Put the butternut squash, carrots and onions on a large baking tray (or two), drizzle with the olive oil, sprinkle with the garlic granules, cumin and paprika, season with salt and pepper and toss well until everything is coated. Roast in the oven for 45 minutes.**

3. **Remove the tray(s) from the oven and add the beetroot, stir gently to coat it in the cooking oils.**

4. **Bake for a further 15 minutes. While the vegetables are cooking, prepare the dressing by whisking all of the ingredients together in a small bowl or jug. Set aside.**

5. **When the vegetables are cooked through, remove from the oven and transfer to a serving dish. Pour over the dressing, toss well and finish with dried cranberries, crumbled feta (if using) and pecans sprinkled over.**

---

**TO MAKE AHEAD**

Roast the vegetables and make the dressing up to 24 hours before serving, chilling them separately until needed. Combine and add the toppings just before serving.

---

**SERVES 6–8 (AS PART OF A BUFFET)**

**1** butternut squash, deseeded and cut into 3cm cubes (no need to peel)
**500g** carrots, peeled and cut into 3cm chunks
**2** red onions, peeled and cut into 3cm chunks
**2 tbsp** olive oil
**2 tsp** garlic granules
**2 tsp** ground cumin
**2 tsp** paprika
**500g** vacuum-packed cooked beetroot (from the supermarket fridge section, not in vinegar), drained and cut into 3cm cubes
sea salt and freshly ground black pepper

**For the Dressing**
**6 tbsp** olive oil (extra virgin if you have it)
**4 tbsp** balsamic vinegar
**3 tbsp** runny honey (or maple syrup)
**2 tsp** Dijon mustard
**½ tsp** sea salt

**To Serve**
**75g** dried cranberries
**100g** feta cheese, crumbled (optional)
**50g** pecan halves

*Cooking for a Crowd*

# CAPRESE-STYLE PASTA SALAD

**15 MINS**

The Italian Caprese-style salad of tomatoes, mozzarella and basil is a pleasing part of a Christmas buffet table, with its jaunty festive colours of red and green. Here I've added pasta to make it a more substantial side dish and pesto and pine nuts to add flavour and texture.

1. **Cook the pasta in salted boiling water according to the packet instructions (about 10 minutes).**

2. **Meanwhile, prepare the rest of the ingredients.**

3. **Drain the cooked pasta and rinse in cold water while it's in the colander to cool it quickly. Be sure the pasta is as dry as possible and place it in a large bowl or serving dish. Add the remaining ingredients and mix well, then season to taste.**

### SERVES 6–8 (AS PART OF A BUFFET)

**300g** dried pasta
**250g** cherry tomatoes, halved
**4** large tomatoes, finely chopped
**½** red onion, peeled and finely chopped
**300g** mini mozzarella balls, drained
**100g** green pesto (or red if you prefer)
**3 tbsp** olive oil
**3 tbsp** balsamic vinegar
**50g** pine nuts, toasted
**15g** fresh basil leaves, shredded
sea salt and freshly ground black pepper

### TO MAKE AHEAD

Prepare and store in the fridge, covered, for up to 24 hours ahead. Stir well before serving.

# CHRISTMAS COLESLAW

**20 MINS**

A classic creamy coleslaw is always a favourite part of a buffet. Here, we've added some extra fruits for a festive flavour. A pot of this in the fridge works brilliantly to turn any leftovers into a meal.

1. **Zest the orange into a large bowl (big enough for all the coleslaw ingredients) and set aside.**

2. **Juice the zested orange into a separate small bowl, add the apple pieces, toss to coat. Allow the apple pieces to sit in the orange juice for 5 minutes.**

3. **To the large bowl with the zest in, add the cabbage, red onion, carrots, mayonnaise, yoghurt, white wine vinegar and sea salt. Mix everything very well to combine. Spoon the soaked apples in to the coleslaw, discard any leftover juice. Mix well.**

4. **Sprinkle with the pomegranate seeds to serve.**

### SERVES 6–8 (AS PART OF A BUFFET)

**1** orange
**2** apples, peeled, cored and cut into 1cm cubes
**½** red cabbage, finely shredded
**½** red onion, peeled and thinly sliced
**150g** carrots, peeled and coarsely grated
**175g** mayonnaise
**100g** Greek yoghurt
**2 tsp** white wine vinegar
**½ tsp** sea salt

**To Serve**
**80g** pomegranate seeds (I use a small prepared pack)

### TO MAKE AHEAD

As the cabbage sits in a dressing, it tends to become watery. I prefer to dress it at the last minute to avoid this. Shred all of the vegetables and make the dressing. Cover and store separately in the fridge for up to 24 hours before serving. Mix and garnish with the pomegranate seeds just before serving.

# DOUGHBALL PLATTER

**V**

**40 MINS, PLUS PROVING TIME**

This is such a fun centrepiece for a New Year's Eve buffet or party. The rolling does take a little while (about 20 minutes) but it's not taxing. Alternatively, if you like the idea but not the kneading and floury work surfaces, you can very happily make this with ready-made pizza dough.

1. Tip the flour, yeast and salt into a bowl and add the oil and water. Use your hands to bring the dough together, then use a stand mixer fitted with the dough hook to knead the dough for 5 minutes on high speed, or knead by hand for 10 minutes, until smooth and springy to the touch.

2. Place the dough in a bowl, cover with oiled cling film and leave to prove at room temperature for 1 hour, until roughly doubled in size.

**MAKES 60 DOUGH BALLS**

**For the Dough**
**500g** strong white bread flour, plus extra for dusting
**7g** sachet fast-action dried yeast
**½ tsp** fine sea salt
**2 tbsp** olive oil, plus extra for greasing
**320ml** lukewarm water

**For the Garlic Butter**
**125g** salted butter, at room temp
**5** garlic cloves, peeled and crushed
**5g** fresh parsley, finely chopped

3. Turn the dough out of the bowl onto a clean, floured surface. Separate it into 60 small dough balls, the easiest way to do this is to cut the dough in half, in half again, and repeat until you make 60 balls. Each ball should weigh about 15g. Use 14–16 dough balls to form each number. Try not to make the balls any bigger than 15g as you will lose the shape of the numbers.

4. Place them on lined baking trays, cover with oiled cling film and leave to prove for a further 30 minutes at room temperature.

5. Make the garlic butter by mashing the ingredients together in a small bowl. Set aside.

6. Preheat the oven to 200°C fan/220°C/Gas Mark 7. Bake the dough balls for 12–15 minutes until just starting to turn golden.

7. When the dough balls are cooked, remove from the tray and serve with the garlic butter (brush it over or serve alongside for dipping, or both).

**TO MAKE AHEAD**

Prep up to step 3, placing the balls on the baking tray and instead of proving a second time, store in the fridge for up to 24 hours, covered with oiled cling film. Bake straight from the fridge.

# CREAMY POTATO GRATIN

**1 HOUR 15 MINS**

Potatoes are one of my love languages. Bathe them in cream with garlic and then we're really talking. The key here is to slice those potatoes really thinly, so they soak up the cream and garlic flavour. This recipe also makes an indulgent alternative to roast potatoes.

1. **Preheat the oven to 160°C fan/180°C/Gas Mark 4 and use the butter to grease the base and sides of the baking dish.**

2. **Lay about a quarter of the potato slices into the bottom of the greased dish. Add a generous sprinkle of salt and pepper and scatter over about a third of the crushed garlic. Repeat the layering until you finish with a layer of potato.**

3. **Mix the cream and milk in a jug. Pour this over the potatoes and bake for 45–60 minutes or until the potatoes are tender and starting to turn brown on top.**

## SERVES 6–8 (AS PART OF A BUFFET)

**30g** salted butter
**1.5kg** white potatoes (I like Maris Piper or King Edward), peeled and very thinly sliced (use a mandoline if you have one)
**4** garlic gloves, peeled and crushed
**300ml** double cream
**300ml** semi-skimmed milk
sea salt and freshly ground black pepper

**You will need:** shallow ovenproof baking dish (about 27 x 20cm)

## TO MAKE AHEAD

If you want to make this in advance, you need to part-bake it and finish off just before you're ready to serve (if you make in advance and leave the potatoes raw, they will discolour). Make up the gratin but use 400ml milk. Cook for 30 minutes. Cool and store in the fridge. When you're ready to serve, bake for 30 minutes, or until the potatoes are tender and the top is golden.

*Cooking for a Crowd*

# PIGS IN BLANKETS SAUSAGE ROLLS

**45 MINS**

My love of a good sausage roll knows no bounds, so it was only a matter of time until this delicious hybrid appeared. We've used prosciutto here rather than regular bacon, as it's thinner and works better hidden beneath the pastry. Don't be tempted to add more cranberry sauce (as I usually am) – it will leak out of the rolls and burn. The poppy seeds are optional, but very pretty.

1. Preheat the oven to 200°C fan/220°C/Gas Mark 7 and line a baking tray with baking paper.

2. Cut the sausages in half widthways and wrap each one in half a prosciutto slice.

3. Unroll the pastry. Position the long side of the pastry towards you and cut it into quarters, then cut each quarter, downwards, to form 3 rectangles.

4. Using a pastry brush, spread the cranberry sauce thinly over the middle of each pastry rectangle. Place a wrapped sausage on to each pastry piece and roll the pastry around it, with the seam pressed firmly underneath.

5. Put the rolls seam side down on the lined baking tray, brush each sausage roll with beaten egg and sprinkle with poppy seeds (if using).

6. Bake in the oven for 30–35 minutes until the pastry is golden and the sausages are cooked through.

## MAKES 12 ROLLS

**400g** pork sausages (about 6)
**84g** prosciutto (6 slices)
**320g** ready-rolled puff pastry sheet
**50g** cranberry sauce (shop-bought or see page 72)
**1** egg, beaten
**2 tsp** poppy seeds (optional)

## TO MAKE AHEAD

Prepare the sausage rolls until the end of step 5. Cover and store in the fridge for up to 3 days, until you're ready to bake. You could also freeze them, uncooked, at the end of step 5, for up to 1 month. Cook as per the instructions, from frozen, allowing an extra 5–10 minutes cooking time to ensure they are cooked through.

# MULLED WINE

## 2 HOURS 5 MINS

Mulled wine is always a festive favourite. Here is my tried and tested method for making it in a slow cooker. The benefit of this is that it can gently warm through, ready to greet you on your arrival at home after a walk or Christmas shopping. You can substitute non-alcoholic wine here if you prefer.

1. **Use a vegetable peeler to peel off the skin of the orange (avoiding the white pith) and put the strips into the slow cooker.**

2. **When you've removed the peel, halve the orange and squeeze all the juice into the slow cooker. Discard the orange shells. Add the remaining ingredients to the slow cooker, pop on the lid and cook on HIGH for 2 hours or LOW for 3–4 hours.**

3. **Before serving, remove the whole spices and orange peel using a sieve or slotted spoon. Add the vanilla, brandy (if using) and fresh orange slices, stir and serve.**

## TO MAKE WITHOUT A SLOW COOKER

Put the orange skin (peeled as above), orange juice, red wine, sugar, cloves, star anise and cinnamon sticks into a saucepan on the hob over a low heat. Allow to warm through for 20–30 minutes. Don't let the mixture boil or you will burn off the alcohol. Finish as step 3 above.

### SERVES 8

**1** orange
**2 x 750ml** bottles of red wine
**125g** soft light brown sugar
**8** whole cloves
**4** star anise
**4** cinnamon sticks

**To Serve**
**2 tsp** vanilla extract
**100ml** brandy (optional)
**1** orange, sliced

### TO MAKE AHEAD

Put the ingredients into the slow cooker, set aside, and cook when you're ready to serve.

Choose a fruity, full-bodied red wine, like a Merlot or Shiraz. If you're vegetarian or vegan, check that the wine is suitable.

# Leftovers

For me, one of the great joys of Christmas is leftovers. What a treat to be greeted by a ready-made buffet every time we open the fridge.

The following recipes are designed to help you use up a range of Christmas leftovers: some are for cooked food and others for surplus ingredients.

Be flexible with what you have to use up and feel free to substitute ingredients and adapt quantities – these recipes are all quite forgiving.

Be mindful of food safety guidance as always:

★ Cool cooked food and refrigerate as quickly as possible, don't leave it to stand at room temperature.

★ When reheating food, ensure it's piping hot throughout and don't reheat more than once.

# LEFTOVER ROOT VEGETABLE SOUP

**35 MINS**

Somehow, no matter how cleverly I plan and shop for Christmas, I always end up with unused vegetables. I panic-buy parsnips in fear of there being a December shortage, I think! Turn any sad-looking forgotten root veg into this simple but tasty soup. You can eat the soup straight away, or freeze it for another day. Serve it with a drizzle of leftover cream, if you have any.

1. **Heat the oil in a saucepan over a medium heat, add the onion, garlic and curry powder and cook gently for 5–10 minutes until the onion has softened. Add the vegetables, stock, salt and some pepper, put the lid on and cook for 25–30 minutes until the vegetables are very soft.**

2. **Remove from the heat and use a hand blender or food processor to blend until smooth.**

3. **Before serving, drizzle with single cream (if using).**

## TO MAKE WITH A SLOW COOKER

Put everything in the slow cooker, use 750ml stock (rather than 1 litre), put the lid on and cook on HIGH for 4–5 hours or LOW for 8–9 hours. Blend to serve.

### SERVES 6

**1 tbsp** olive oil
**1** onion, peeled and chopped
**3** garlic cloves, peeled and crushed
**1 tbsp** medium curry powder
**800g** uncooked root vegetables (like parsnips and carrots), peeled and cut into 2cm cubes
**1 litre** hot chicken or vegetable stock (made from a cube is fine)
**1 tsp** sea salt
freshly ground black pepper

**To Serve**
**2 tbsp** single cream (optional)

**You will need:** stick blender or food processor

### TO MAKE AHEAD

This soup freezes well. Cool and split into portions. Defrost and heat thoroughly on the hob or in the microwave.

# ONE-POT BOXING DAY PIE

**30 MINS**

If you're all cooked out after the big day, this is the recipe for you. It uses an instant sauce that cooks and thickens in the oven, there's no stirring and it's ready in 30 minutes. Relax and enjoy Boxing Day comfort food!

1. **Preheat the oven to 180°C fan/200°C/Gas Mark 6.**

2. **Make the sauce first. Put the cornflour in a small bowl, add a spoon or two of the stock and stir until it forms a smooth paste (it's important to make this cornflour 'paste' so that the sauce doesn't go lumpy). Add the paste to the rest of the stock and combine with the cream, mustard and plenty of salt and pepper. Mix well.**

3. **Put all the chopped meat and vegetables in the roasting or pie dish and pour over the sauce. Carefully top with the pastry. Brush the pastry with the beaten egg, prick a few holes in the top and bake in the oven for 20–25 minutes, until the pastry is golden on top and the meats inside are hot through.**

4. **Remove from the oven and serve.**

| SERVES 6 |
| --- |

**500–600g** leftover cooked turkey, pigs in blankets or ham, cut into bite-sized pieces
**500–600g** leftover cooked vegetables and/or stuffing, cut into bite-sized pieces
**320g** ready-rolled puff pastry sheet
**1** egg, beaten

**For the Sauce**
**50g** cornflour
**250ml** hot chicken stock (made from a cube is fine)
**300ml** single cream
**2 tsp** wholegrain mustard
sea salt and freshly ground black pepper

**You will need:** shallow roasting or pie dish (about 20 x 25cm)

# LEFTOVER TURKEY CURRY

**55 MINS**

For those of us of a certain age, a turkey curry is impossible to think of without imagining Bridget Jones's mother's buffet, but please don't let that put you off! I look forward to this recipe every festive season, I think it's something to do with the welcome change of flavours from the week before. This has lots of extra goodness, with lentils and a couple of portions of vegetables also included.

1. **Heat the oil in a large saucepan over a medium heat, add the onions, garlic, ginger and curry paste and cook gently for about 10 minutes until soft. Add the butternut squash, tomatoes, stock, lentils and salt, stir well and pop a lid on. Cook for 15–25 minutes, stirring occasionally.**

2. **When the lentils and butternut squash are soft and cooked through, add the turkey and chutney. Cook for a further 5–10 minutes until the turkey is hot through.**

3. **Turn off the heat, add the spinach and cover for 5 minutes until wilted. Mix and serve.**

## TO MAKE WITH A SLOW COOKER

Put everything in the slow cooker, apart from the cooked turkey, spinach and mango chutney. Put the lid on and cook on HIGH for 5–6 hours or LOW for 8–9 hours. Add the turkey, pop the lid back on and cook on HIGH for 30 minutes until heated through. Add the spinach and mango chutney before serving (the heat of the curry will wilt the spinach).

| SERVES 6 |
| --- |

**2 tsp** olive oil
**2** onions, peeled and finely chopped
**4** garlic cloves, peeled and crushed
**1 tbsp** ginger purée (or fresh grated ginger if you prefer)
**150g** curry paste (see Notes below)
**500g** butternut squash cubes (see Notes below)
**1 x 400g** tin chopped tomatoes
**500ml** hot vegetable stock (made from a cube is fine)
**100g** dried red lentils, rinsed
**½ tsp** sea salt
**500g** leftover cooked turkey, cut into 3cm chunks
**4 tbsp** mango chutney
**200g** baby spinach

Use a curry paste to suit your own tastes and spice level (such as korma, or tikka masala). Check the packet for what is considered a serving for 6 people and adjust the amount in the recipe accordingly. It's usually 1–2 tablespoons per person but it may vary for different brands.

I use a 500g bag of frozen prepared butternut squash here as it's such a handy shortcut. If you prefer to use fresh, that's fine. A small butternut squash will be about 500g after peeling and deseeding.

# BOXING DAY FRITTATA

**20 MINS**

A frittata takes a box of eggs and turns it into a complete meal in less than half an hour. This dish is perfect served as brunch, lunch or dinner. We're using up some of our leftover cooked vegetables, but it's also a handy way to use up some leftover cheese too. Carrots, parsnips and potatoes work particularly well in this, you can also add leftover cooked ham or turkey. I tend to avoid adding cooked red cabbage as it will turn the frittata pink!

1.  Heat the oil in a large ovenproof frying pan over a medium heat. Add the vegetables and season with plenty of salt and pepper. Add the eggs and pesto to a separate bowl and beat gently. Pour the beaten eggs over the vegetables and sprinkle over the cheese. Reduce the heat to low and cook for 5–10 minutes, or until the edges of the frittata have started to set.

2.  Meanwhile, preheat the grill to high.

3.  Transfer the frying pan from the hob to the grill to cook the top of the frittata: let it grill for about 5 minutes until the top is set and golden – if you prod the middle with a knife there should be no liquid egg.

4.  Cut into wedges to serve.

**SERVES 4**

**2 tsp** sunflower oil
**500–600g** leftover cooked vegetables, roughly chopped
**6** eggs, beaten
**2 tsp** green pesto
**100g** Cheddar cheese, grated (or other leftover cheese)
sea salt and freshly ground black pepper

Leftover frittata can be served cold another time.

# CHEESE & CHUTNEY SCONES

**20 MINS**

These are based on a recipe that my grandma, Ivy, gave me 30 years ago. They are one of my favourite ways to use up leftover hard cheeses and they work particularly well with those strong cheeses we all enjoy at this time of year. You can add a handful of leftover chopped nuts and fruits if you have any left from your cheeseboard.

1. **Preheat the oven as high as it will go – usually 220°C fan/240°C/Gas Mark 9 – and line a baking tray with baking paper.**

2. **Put the flour, baking powder and salt into a mixing bowl. Add the butter and rub it in with your fingertips (loosely lift some of the butter with the flour mixture and rub it between the tips of your thumb and fingers to break the butter into smaller pieces) until it looks like lumpy sand. This will take about 5 minutes. Add half the grated cheese and the chutney, stir gently, then add the milk. Use your hands to gently bring it all together into a ball of dough.**

3. **Lightly dust the work surface and a rolling pin with flour. Roll out or pat the dough with your hands to slightly flatten it to a thickness of 2.5–3cm. Cut out 8 round circles using a 7cm round cutter or upturned glass.**

4. **Pop the scones onto the lined baking tray, brush the tops with beaten egg and sprinkle over the remaining cheese. Bake in the oven for 10 minutes, or until risen and golden.**

5. **Scones are best served fresh on the day you bake them. If you want to serve them the next day, toast and fill with bacon for breakfast. (They also freeze well, but why deny yourself that bacon-filled joy.)**

---

### MAKES 8 BIG SCONES

**500g** plain flour, plus extra for dusting
**1 tbsp** baking powder
**1 tsp** fine sea salt
**80g** salted butter, straight from the fridge, cut into chunks
**200g** mature Cheddar cheese (or any other leftover cheese, see Note), grated
**3 tbsp** chutney of choice (use leftovers from a jar or your own homemade chutney on page 178)
**250ml** whole milk
**1** egg, beaten

**You will need:** 7cm round cutter (optional – you could just use an upturned glass)

If your leftover cheese is a hard type, grate it. If it is softer, crumble it using your fingers or finely chop it into very small cubes

# CHOCOLATE SALAMI

**30 MINS, PLUS CHILLING TIME**

If you have leftover chocolate or biscuits after Christmas and fancy combining them, this is the perfect recipe. This is a version of an Italian treat, which is traditionally served sliced after dinner with coffee. This recipe would also make a super homemade gift, perhaps tied with string to give the effect of a real salami!

1. Put the butter in a large saucepan over the lowest heat for 5 minutes, or until it begins to melt. Now add the chopped chocolate, stirring regularly until melted (it's important to keep the heat low here so that you don't burn the chocolate).

2. Remove the pan from the heat and stir in the milk, beating well to combine. Add the biscuits, cranberries and nuts. Mix everything until totally combined.

3. Lay two large pieces of cling film on top of one another so you have a double thickness. Tip the mixture onto the middle and form it into a log shape. You are aiming for your log to be 6–7cm thick and 12cm long. Use the cling film to roll it up and twist the ends into a sausage shape.

4. Transfer to the fridge to set for at least 4 hours.

5. Remove from the fridge, unwrap and roll in sifted icing sugar until completely coated. Cut into about ten 1–2cm-thick slices using a very sharp knife. Hold your hand around the salami and use a sawing motion to cut – this helps to avoid breakages (if it's too hard to cut, allow it to come to room temperature slightly).

| MAKES 10 SLICES |
| --- |

**100g** salted butter
**200g** milk chocolate, chopped
**2 tbsp** milk
(whole or semi-skimmed)
**75g** rich tea biscuits (or similar),
broken into pieces
**50g** dried cranberries
**75g** nuts, roughly chopped
(salted or unsalted is fine)
**2 tbsp** icing sugar, sifted

Store in the fridge for up to 5 days.

# CHRISTMAS BROWNIES

**35 MINS, PLUS COOLING TIME**

Christmas in our house always includes a tub of Cadbury's Heroes, Celebrations or Quality Street. They live in our sitting room and wink at me every time I am on the sofa. The discussion about which is our favourite keeps going throughout the festive period, and there are always a handful left. This recipe is a delicious way to make the most of any leftover chocolates.

1. Preheat the oven to 180°C fan/200°C/Gas Mark 6 and line the base and sides of the tin or dish with baking paper.

2. Heat the butter in a saucepan over a very low heat. When it's starting to melt, add the dark chocolate and the sugar. Stir until everything is melted together, then remove from the heat and leave to cool for 5–10 minutes.

3. Beat in the eggs, one by one, then stir in the flour. Stir half of the chocolates into the brownie batter, pour it into the lined tin or dish and top with the remaining chocolates.

4. Bake in the oven for 20–25 minutes, or until the edges are just solid but the middle still has a little wobble. Be careful not to overbake the mix! Brownies are better slightly underdone than over.

5. Remove from the oven and allow to cool completely (if you can bear it!) before cutting into 16 pieces.

### MAKES 16 PIECES

**125g** unsalted butter
**150g** dark chocolate (about 70% cocoa solids), broken into pieces
**150g** soft light brown sugar
**2** eggs
**90g** plain flour
**300g** Cadbury Miniature Heroes (or other assorted chocolates), unwrapped

**You will need:** 20cm square baking tin or dish

Store in an airtight container for up to 5 days.

# Desserts

There's always space for festive dessert!

I have never knowingly under-catered when it comes to desserts – I can't resist a showstopper.

If you are a guest travelling with a pudding made at home, I would recommend taking the individual components separately and finishing the dessert when you arrive at your destination, just before serving. This minimises stress and chance of disaster. So, for example, leave your cheesecake in the tin or pack the wreath pavlova and cream separately.

These recipes are all designed and tested to be suitable for preparing in advance, and all, apart from the Slow Cooker Chocolate Orange Pudding, can be halved if you prefer.

# WREATH PAVLOVA

## 1 HOUR 20 MINS, PLUS COOLING TIME

This decadent, fruity dessert is perfect after a rich Christmas meal. Meringue-making can be a little intimidating, but the tips below should help to avoid any panic and will result in a perfect pavlova. You can also make the pavlova base well in advance, so you have it done and ready to go on the day.

1. Preheat the oven to 140°C fan/160°C/Gas Mark 3.

2. **Draw a wreath shape on a sheet of baking paper or baking parchment (NOT greaseproof paper) using a pencil. Start by drawing around the outside of a small dinner plate to make the outside edge. Now use a small glass or ramekin to mark the inside circle. Flip the paper over (so the egg mixture doesn't touch the pencil marks) and sit it on a baking tray.**

3. **Now make the meringue. Whisk the egg whites in a very clean bowl with a hand-held electric whisk or stand mixer fitted with the whisk attachment until they form stiff peaks, then gradually add the sugar, a little at a time, whisking well in between each addition.**

4. **Use a tiny dot or two of the egg white mixture to 'glue' the paper to the baking tray. Spoon dollops of meringue mix onto the template and smooth the top so it has a slightly flat surface. Bake in the oven for 50–60 minutes until the meringue looks dry and crisp. Turn off the oven and leave the meringue to cool in the oven (this helps to avoid it cracking).**

5. **Meanwhile, make the sauce. Mash the raspberries and then squish through a sieve into a bowl, discard the seeds left in the sieve. Stir in the icing sugar.**

6. **For the topping, whisk the double cream in a bowl with the icing sugar until it forms soft peaks.**

7. **When ready to serve, top the meringue with cream topping, fresh fruit, sauce and some mint sprigs (if using).**

### SERVES 8

**For the Meringue**
4 egg whites
250g caster sugar

**For the Sauce**
150g raspberries (fresh, or frozen and defrosted)
2 tbsp icing sugar, sifted

**For the Topping**
300ml double cream
2 tbsp icing sugar, sifted
150g fresh cherries
80g pomegranate seeds (I use a prepared pack)
225g fresh raspberries
fresh mint, to garnish (optional)

**You will need:** hand-held electric whisk or stand mixer fitted with whisk attachment

### TO MAKE AHEAD

After your meringue has cooled, store in an airtight container (like a cake tin or plastic storage box) at room temperature for up to a week. Prepare the sauce and the toppings and finish just before serving.

# ZESTY LEMON POTS

**20 MINS, PLUS COOLING TIME**

This is a version of the old English dessert, lemon posset. Ridiculously simple to make and utterly decadent, I've added oranges to the classic recipe for some extra festive flavours. The portions are small as it's very rich: serve it in your smallest glasses or some ramekins.

1. Heat the cream, sugar and citrus zest (reserving half the orange zest to serve) in a large saucepan over a medium heat, stirring gently. Bring to the boil and let the cream bubble for 1 minute, then remove from the heat.

2. Meanwhile, use the zested fruits to make up the required amount of juice. Stir the juice into the cream mix and mix well.

3. Pour into individual glasses or ramekins, carefully cover and pop into the fridge for at least 2 hours or better still, overnight.

4. Just before serving, sprinkle over the extra orange zest.

### MAKES 6 SMALL GLASSES OR RAMEKINS

**900ml** double cream
**250g** caster sugar
**2** lemons, zested
**2** oranges, zested
**150ml** juice (made up about 50/50 lemon and orange, using the zested fruits)

### TO MAKE AHEAD

Make the pots up to 2 days in advance and store in the fridge until ready to serve.

*Desserts*

# CHOCOLATE ORANGE PUDDING

**2 HOURS 5 MINS**

This recipe is one of the most popular Christmas recipes I've ever shared online. I think part of its charm is the need to suspend disbelief, as it looks like a disaster before it's cooked! Then you dive into the finished product and discover the magic molten chocolate sauce hiding below the sponge – a joy.

1. **Grease the slow cooker bowl thoroughly with the 20g butter.**

2. **In a large bowl, make the pudding mix. Mix the melted butter, flour, sugar, cocoa, baking powder, eggs, milk and orange extract together until smooth. Put into the greased slow cooker bowl and even out the top. Add most of the chocolate orange segments evenly on top, pressing them into the mixture (keep a few segments back for decoration at the end).**

3. **Mix the sugar and cocoa powder for the topping in a small bowl, then sprinkle it evenly over the top of the pudding mix.**

4. **Carefully pour over the boiling water (It will all look a bit odd at the moment, but keep the faith!). Put the lid on the slow cooker and cook on HIGH for 1–2 hours until the pudding is firm in the middle.**

5. **Take off the lid and sit your reserved pieces of chocolate orange on top to decorate, put the lid back on and cook for a further 30 minutes, then serve.**

6. **Keep leftovers in the fridge and re-heat in the microwave (or serve cold) for pudding the next day.**

## TO MAKE WITHOUT A SLOW COOKER

Make as above in a shallow baking dish (about 27 x 20cm) and bake at 160°C fan/180°C/Gas Mark 4, covered in foil, for 30–40 minutes.

### SERVES 8

**20g** unsalted butter, at room temperature, for greasing

**For the Pudding**
**100g** unsalted butter, melted
**250g** self-raising flour
**125g** soft light brown sugar
**30g** good-quality cocoa powder
**1 tsp** baking powder
**3 eggs**
**150ml** milk (whole or semi-skimmed)
**2 tsp** orange extract
**157g** Terry's Chocolate Orange (or other orange-flavoured chocolate), roughly chopped

**For the Topping**
**150g** soft light brown sugar
**20g** good-quality cocoa powder
**500ml** boiling water

### TO MAKE AHEAD

If you're short on time, you can mix up the sponge batter and leave in the fridge overnight before adding the toppings and baking the following day. This method does give a slightly less fluffy sponge, but it's still delicious.

*Desserts*

# VERY BERRY TRIFLE

**1 HOUR, PLUS CHILLING TIME**

For many families, Christmas trifle is a must-have retro classic. My version is taken up a notch as I make my own custard: you don't need to (you can use a 500-g carton of ready-made custard if you prefer) but if you fancy having a go, I promise it's not too tricky and it's so worth it. Just be patient, stir it over a very gentle heat, and you'll be rewarded!

1. **Put 100g of the frozen raspberries in the bottom of the trifle bowl, plus 150g of the halved strawberries, arranging the cut edges of the strawberries against the side of the bowl.**

2. **Dissolve the jelly cubes in the boiling water in a heatproof bowl, then add a further 100ml cold water. Mix until dissolved. Pour the jelly over the fruit and refrigerate for about 3 hours, until completely set.**

3. **While the jelly sets, make the custard. Put the egg yolks into a heatproof bowl, add the cornflour and caster sugar, and whisk together, adding a tablespoon or two of the milk to form a smooth paste.**

4. **Heat the remaining milk, along with the vanilla extract, in a small saucepan over a medium heat until it is just starting to bubble on the surface. Slowly and carefully, pour the hot milk into the egg yolk mixture, whisking continuously as you add it, until you have a smooth mixture.**

5. **Return the mixture to the pan over a low-medium heat, cook for 5–10 minutes, whisking gently, until very thick. Remove from the heat and whisk in the cream.**

6. **Cover the surface of the custard with a sheet of cling film (press it against the surface of the custard so it doesn't form a skin), allow the custard to cool to room temperature, then put it in the fridge.**

**SERVES 8–10**

**300g** frozen raspberries
**400g** strawberries, hulled and halved lengthways
**½** pack raspberry-flavour jelly (cubes not powder – about 70g)
**150ml** boiling water
**15g** caster sugar

**For the Custard**
**4** egg yolks
**55g** cornflour
**75g** caster sugar
**450ml** whole milk
**2 tsp** vanilla extract
**150ml** double cream

**To Assemble**
**450ml** double cream
**50g** icing sugar
**25g** flaked almonds
**175g** shop-bought Swiss roll, cut into 2cm-thick slices

**You will need:** trifle bowl

7.  While the jelly and custard are chilling, put the remaining raspberries in a small bowl, add the caster sugar, mash together and set aside. (If the raspberries are not yet thawed, leave them to melt slightly.)

8.  Whisk the double cream in a bowl with the icing sugar until it forms soft peaks.

9.  Toast the flaked almonds in a small frying pan over a medium heat for 4–5 minutes until coloured but not burned (keep an eye on them!). Set aside to cool.

10. When the jelly is set, remove it from the fridge, sit the slices of Swiss roll on top, flat side down, and spoon over the mashed raspberries. Place the remaining strawberries around the edges of the bowl with the cut sides against the sides of the bowl.

11. Spoon over the custard and smooth out. Spoon the cream on top and sprinkle over the toasted almonds.

12. Store in the fridge until ready to serve.

**TO MAKE AHEAD**

Finish the trifle at the custard layer, cover and store in the fridge for up to 2 days until you're ready to serve. Top with the cream and nuts up to 2 hours before serving and return to the fridge.

If serving to vegetarians, check the jelly you are using is suitable.

The leftover egg whites can be used for the pavlova on page 150.

# TIPS FOR A TERRIFIC TRIFLE

If you have time, make your trifle the day before serving and
store it in the fridge. This gives it time to set well and for all of
the fruity flavours to blend together.

It's worth taking the time to toast your flaked almonds,
it adds colour and flavour.

Don't forget to use cling film pressed down onto the top of
the custard as it cools. This avoids the custard developing a 'skin'
on top which will cause lumps.

If you're using a glass dish and you want to form the neat layers
around the outside, you may need to slightly adjust the quantities of ingredients
for each layer/component to fit your own trifle bowl.

If you wanted to make extra custard to serve on Christmas day
with a dessert, just double the recipe and store half in the fridge
(with the cling film on the surface) for up to 2 days. Reheat very gently
in a pan on the hob before serving.

# VEGAN BLACK FOREST TART

**35 MINS, PLUS CHILLING TIME**

Whether you're vegan or not, this rich and decadent tart is a totally delicious end to any meal. If your flan tin is smaller than the one I use here, you may end up with leftover filling. If you do, spoon this into small glasses and serve it as mousse!

1. Remove the cherries from the freezer and set aside to defrost while you make the tart base.

2. Line the base of the flan tin with baking paper. Combine the crushed biscuits with the melted plant-based spread and press into the tin, then chill in the fridge for 1 hour.

3. Put the chopped chocolate in a large heatproof bowl.

4. Warm the coconut milk and sugar in a pan, scraping down the sides of the tin to get all of the thickened cream out. It may look lumpy, but whisk and cook for 5 minutes until bubbling and it will become smooth.

5. Pour the coconut milk over the chopped chocolate and leave to stand for 5 minutes, then mix well to ensure all of the chocolate has melted. Stir in the vanilla extract.

6. Use a sieve to strain the defrosted cherries, gently pressing to remove any excess juice, and discard the liquid. Spread the cherries evenly over the chilled biscuit base.

7. Pour the chocolate and cream mixture over the cherries and chill in the fridge for at least 4 hours (or overnight if you can).

8. Whip the cream in a bowl until if forms soft peaks, then pour over the middle of the chocolate tart. Decorate with the fresh cherries and some of the grated dark chocolate, and serve.

## SERVES 12

**For the Base**
**400g** Oreos, crushed
**75g** plant-based spread, melted

**For the Filling**
**480g** bag frozen cherries
**400g** dark chocolate (70% cocoa solids and suitable for vegans), finely chopped
**1 x 400ml** tin coconut milk (NOT reduced fat)
**50g** soft light brown sugar
**1 tsp** vanilla extract

**To Decorate**
**220ml** plant-based whipping cream alternative
**200g** fresh cherries
Dark chocolate, grated

**You will need:** 25cm round, loose-bottomed flan tin (ideally at least 5.5cm deep)

### TO MAKE AHEAD

This tart can be made and refrigerated for up to 2 days before adding the cream. Add the cream on top and fresh cherries just before serving.

It can be quite difficult to remove this from the base of the tin. If you have any problems lifting the tart out, just serve it on the base of the loose-bottomed tin.

# NO BAKE CHOCO-NUT CHEESECAKE

**30 MINS, PLUS CHILLING TIME**

There's something utterly festive about Ferrero Rocher, the gold foil-wrapped hazelnut chocolates. This recipe uses them (or another similar chocolate) to create a rich but very simple-to-make cheesecake. With this dessert, the Ambassador will be really spoiling us!

1. Combine the crushed biscuits with the melted butter and press into the tin.

2. Melt the 300g of milk chocolate for the cheesecake in a microwaveable bowl in the microwave in 30-second bursts (mixing well after each burst, even if it doesn't look like it needs it). Alternatively, melt the chocolate in a small heatproof bowl set over a pan of simmering water (do not let the bottom of the bowl touch the water, and stir occasionally until the chocolate melts). Set the melted chocolate aside for 5 minutes until it cools to room temperature.

3. Pour the double cream into a large clean bowl, add the cream cheese and icing sugar and beat until very stiff and thick (use an electric hand whisk if you have one). It's ready when it's the consistency of ice cream.

4. Add the cooled melted chocolate and crushed hazelnut chocolates and beat until well combined. Spoon the cheesecake mixture on top of the biscuit base, smoothing the top, and transfer to the fridge for 4 hours (or longer) to set.

5. Remove from the fridge, run a knife around the edge of the tin and gently push the cheesecake out (if it's a loose-bottom type, you can sit it on a glass or can and gently push the sides of the tin downwards to help).

6. Melt the remaining chocolate (using the method explained above) and drizzle over the cheesecake. Top with the remaining hazelnut chocolates. Add sprinkles if you fancy.

---

### SERVES 12

**For the Base**
**200g** digestive biscuits, crushed
**100g** unsalted butter, melted

**For the Cheesecake Mixture**
**300g** milk chocolate, broken
  into pieces
**500ml** double cream,
  at room temperature
**500g** full-fat cream cheese,
  at room temperature
**75g** icing sugar
**250g** hazelnut chocolates
  (such as Ferrero Rocher)

**To Decorate**
**100g** milk chocolate,
  broken into pieces
**12** hazelnut chocolates
  (such as Ferrero Rocher)
edible gold sprinkles (optional)

**You will need:** 18cm round loose-bottomed cake tin (the type with deep sides)

---

### TO MAKE AHEAD
Prepare the cheesecake up to the end of step 4. Keep it in the fridge in the tin for up to 2 days. When you're ready to serve, or up to 2 hours before, finish the cheesecake as per the final steps.

# CHRISTMAS TIRAMISU

**45 MINS**

A good tiramisu is a true joy. Don't be put off by the raw eggs: I promise, they make the dish. In fact, a true tiramisu has no cream at all, the filling mix is just mascarpone, sugar and eggs. I have used some artistic license here and included cream so it's a little more accessible, but every bit as delicious. If you are serving this to pregnant people, young children, or anyone at risk, you can leave out the eggs, but I have to say, it won't be a patch on the original, the cream will have more of a cheesecake texture.

1. **Make the coffee up with the boiling water and add the liqueur. Set aside to cool.**

2. **Whisk the eggs and sugar in a large, clean bowl until foamy (if you are using an electric mixer this should take around 5 minutes; it will take longer if whisked by hand). Set aside.**

3. **In a second bowl, whisk the mascarpone, cream and vanilla until thick and stiff (use an electric hand whisk if you have one, it will be much quicker). Stir in the orange zest and juice.**

4. **Spoon about a third of the mascarpone and cream mixture into the bowl with the eggs and whisk until combined. Add the mascarpone and egg mixture back into the bowl of cream and fold in carefully until there are no lumps (we are trying to keep the air in the mixture so it has a light and fluffy texture).**

5. **To assemble the tiramisu, pour the coffee mixture into a shallow bowl, then really carefully dip in half of the panettone slices, immersing them on both sides (be super quick here – only around 2 seconds for each side – otherwise the panettone will break up) and lay these in the trifle dish. Add half the cream mixture, then repeat with another layer of panettone slices, and again top with the cream. Carefully grate the dark chocolate over the top of the cream, cover and chill until ready to serve.**

## SERVES 12

**4 tsp** instant coffee granules
**150ml** boiling water
**50ml** triple sec or orange liqueur (such as Cointreau)
**2** eggs
**100g** caster sugar
**2 x 250g** tubs mascarpone
**600ml** double cream
**2 tsp** vanilla extract
**1** orange, zested and juiced
**500g** panettone (I use chocolate panettone cut into 2cm-thick slices)
**20g** dark chocolate

**You will need:** trifle bowl

### TO MAKE AHEAD
The tiramisu will keep in the fridge for up to 2 days before serving.

If you can only find plain panettone this will still work, but I would add in extra grated chocolate in the layers.

# HOW TO MAKE A BRILLIANT CHEESEBOARD

For me, a definite highlight of Christmas Day is a beautiful cheeseboard. Everyone groans and says they couldn't possibly eat another thing and then has a nibble or two. That's fine, we can happily graze on it until New Year. Below is the framework that I loosely use when shopping for a cheeseboard, but of course, shop to the tastes of your own guests. The magic here is laying it out to look as bountiful as possible. Use a tray or board slightly smaller than you think you need, so that everything looks full and overflowing.

## BASIC CHEESES

1 strong-flavoured hard cheese (like a mature Cheddar or Comté) ☐

1 lighter-flavoured, softer-textured cheese (like a goat's cheese and/or brie) ☐

1 blue cheese, if you are a fan (like Roquefort or Stilton) ☐

## EXTRA CHEESES

a cheese with extra flavours (like a smoked cheese or a truffle cheese) ☐

a cheese with fruit (like Wensleydale with cranberries) ☐

a goat or sheep's milk cheese (if you don't already have one in your basic cheeses) ☐

## ACCOMPANIMENTS

3 types of crackers (I like to include a variety of shapes and colours) ☐

3 types of fresh sides (grapes, celery, sliced pears or apples, gherkins) ☐

2 types of nuts and/or dried fruit (I LOVE Marcona almonds or dried figs) ☐

2 'sauces' (chutney from a jar, homemade chutney from page 178, honey also works well with many cheeses) ☐

fresh herbs to garnish (rosemary and thyme work well) ☐

# TO PUT YOUR CHEESEBOARD TOGETHER

Choose a tray, chopping board or serving platter. I sometimes add a sheet of baking paper to the board to add interest (this also makes the clean-up easier!)

Lay your cheeses on the board.

Surround the cheeses with rows of crackers.

Add small pots of the 'sauces'.

Add the fresh elements of your board, dotting them around the crackers.

Finish with nuts and dried fruit to fill in the gaps.

If you're using fresh herbs, tuck them into any spaces to garnish.

Cover well and store in the fridge until you're ready (if you don't have space for the board in the fridge, make this up an hour before serving).

Let your cheese come to room temperature, remove it from the fridge about an hour before serving.

## HOW MUCH CHEESE?

If you're serving your cheeseboard after dinner, Paxton and Whitfield suggest 80g of cheese per person, so for 6 people, about 750g cheese in total.

If you're serving your cheeseboard as the main event for a cheese buffet, plan for about 200g per person. I'd also suggest adding some charcuterie, salami, ham etc., for this board.

## NOTE FOR VEGETARIANS OR VEGANS

If you are serving guests who are vegetarian, please check the individual cheeses and the preferences of your guests, as many cheeses are not suitable for vegetarians. If you have vegan guests, there are some good vegan cheese alternatives available, try La Fauxmagerie by mail-order.

# Homemade Gifts

Any homemade gift is a treat to receive,
but even more so if it's edible!

There are recipes in this chapter to suit many tastes;
sweet, savoury, vegan or vegetarian, along with quick
recipes and make ahead options.

I like to stock up on some cellophane bags and ribbon,
along with brown parcel tags, for parcelling up any
homemade treat to make it look extra special.

# CANDY CANE FUDGE

**10 MINS, PLUS OVERNIGHT SETTING TIME**

This method of making fudge is my go-to for easy homemade gifts. Once chilled and cut, it looks far more impressive than the ten minutes it takes to make. Technically it's not real fudge as it doesn't involve boiling sugar, but it's every bit as delicious. Here, I've added mint flavouring and candy canes to give it a festive flavour and colour. This is very easy to make a vegan version of for gifts (see page 213).

1. **Line the base and sides of the tin with baking paper.**

2. **Put the chocolate, condensed milk and peppermint extract in a large microwaveable bowl and microwave in 30-second bursts (mixing well after each burst, even if it looks like it doesn't look like it needs it). Alternatively, melt the chocolate in a heatproof bowl set over a pan of simmering water (do not let the bottom of the bowl touch the water, and stir occasionally until the chocolate melts).**

3. **Pour into the lined tin, smooth out and quickly sprinkle with chopped candy canes. Take a fresh piece of baking paper and use it to press down carefully all over the surface of the fudge so the candy canes are firmly indented into the fudge.**

4. **Refrigerate overnight to set (first removing the piece of paper you used to press it).**

5. **Turn out the fudge, remove the paper and cut the fudge into 36 small chunks.**

## TO MAKE WITH A SLOW COOKER

Put the chocolate, condensed milk and peppermint extract into the slow cooker pot, give everything a good stir, put the lid on and cook on LOW for 30 minutes, stirring very well every 10 minutes. When the fudge is thick and smooth, continue from step 3 above.

---

**MAKES 36 CHUNKS**

**400g** dark chocolate (50–55% cocoa solids), broken into small pieces

**1 x 397g** tin condensed milk

**2 tsp** peppermint extract

**50g** candy canes, cut into very small pieces

**You will need:** 20cm square baking tin or dish

Store in the fridge for up to 1 week.

# CHRISTMAS POPCORN SLAB

**20 MINS, PLUS CHILLING TIME**

Popcorn is surprisingly easy to make at home and is one of those things that really is so much better fresh from the pan. (Although you can easily make this from step 3 with ready-popped popcorn from a bag if you prefer – it will still be delicious.) Portioned into small cellophane bags this makes a fun gift for the lucky recipient to nibble on while watching a Christmas film.

1. Heat the oil in a saucepan over a medium heat and add the popcorn kernels. Put the lid on quickly! Leave the lid on and wait for the popping to start. Once it starts, it will pop almost continuously for 5–10 minutes. During this time, carefully use a tea towel to hold the lid down and shake the pan once or twice.

2. When the popping slows down to only one pop every 4 or 5 seconds, turn off the heat. Remove the lid and set aside for 5 minutes.

3. While the popcorn is cooling, melt the white chocolate: place it in a microwavable bowl and microwave in 30-second bursts (mixing well after each burst, even if it looks like it doesn't look like it needs it). Alternatively, melt the chocolate in a heatproof bowl set over a pan of simmering water (do not let the bottom of the bowl touch the water, and stir occasionally until the chocolate melts).

4. Spread the popped corn on a large baking tray and sprinkle over the melted chocolate, pretzels and sprinkles. Pop into the fridge for 1 hour until the chocolate is set. Separate any big chunks and serve.

### SERVES 6

**2 tbsp** sunflower oil
**100g** popcorn kernels
(the yellow un-popped type)
**300g** white chocolate, cut into
small pieces
**100g** salted pretzels
**50g** edible Christmas sprinkles

### TO MAKE AHEAD

When set, store in a sealed tin in a cool place for up to 5 days.

# PESTO PARMESAN STRAWS

**25 MINS**

I've never met a cheese straw I didn't like, and these are no exception. I've used the shortcut of ready-rolled puff pastry – I try to buy the 'all butter' version for these as it adds to the flavour. Cook these really well so they are crispy and crunchy, making them easier to handle when you package them up as gifts.

1. **Preheat the oven to 200°C fan/220°C/Gas Mark 7and line a baking tray with baking paper.**

2. **Unroll the puff pastry sheet and cut it in half, so you can sandwich both sides together (like closing a book). Spread the pesto all over the surface of one half and sprinkle with 50g of the grated Parmesan. Sit the other half of the pastry on top and press down firmly, then cut the pastry into 16 x 1cm-thick strips (if you have a pizza cutter then use it here as it will make cutting the strips much easier). It will help if you wipe the knife or cutter between each slice.**

3. **Carefully pick up each straw, holding at each end and twist gently. Place the twisted straws on the lined baking tray and brush the tops with the beaten egg.**

4. **Sprinkle over the remaining 25g of Parmesan over the top of the straws and bake in the oven for 8–10 minutes or until crispy and golden all over.**

5. **Remove from the oven and serve warm or at room temperature.**

| MAKES 16 |
| --- |

**320g** ready-rolled puff pastry sheet (ideally all-butter)
**2 tbsp** pesto (green or red)
**75g** Parmesan cheese, grated
**1** egg, beaten

| TO MAKE AHEAD |
| --- |

Make and keep in the fridge, uncooked, for 24 hours. Alternatively, store cooked in an airtight container for up to 2 days.

If serving to vegetarians, use a suitable Parmesan alternative.

# SLOW COOKER
# RED ONION CHUTNEY

## 12 HOURS 10 MINUTES

The time of year when we are all enjoying cheeseboards is the perfect time to try your hand at making chutney. This method is super simple, no worrying about burning sugar like making traditional chutney. For a shortcut, use ready-sliced red onions from the supermarket.

1. **Put all the ingredients in the slow cooker and cook on HIGH for about 12 hours with the lid slightly ajar until the onions are very soft and dark.**

2. **Pour into three clean lidded jam jars (or other containers). Seal and, when cool, put in the fridge.**

### TO MAKE WITHOUT A SLOW COOKER

Cook the ingredients above, along with 4 tablespoons of water, in a heavy saucepan over a low heat, without a lid, for 1½–2 hours, stirring regularly.

---

### MAKES 3 MEDIUM JAM JARS

**1kg** red onions, peeled, halved and thinly sliced
**1 tbsp** mixed spice
**150g** soft light brown sugar
**75ml** red wine vinegar

**You will need:** 3 medium jam jars

Store in the fridge for
up to 4 weeks.

# GINGERBREAD ROCKY ROAD

**15 MINS, PLUS CHILLING TIME**

When you're short on time, rocky road is such a handy no-bake treat. It's mixed up in less than 15 minutes, and this one is packed with heaps of festive flavours. Despite how easy it is to put together, a plate piled with cubes of this never fails to impress. Cut it small, it's very rich! Most supermarket bakery sections have mini gingerbread men at this time of year, but if you can't find them you can just use extra crumbled gingernut biscuits.

1. **Line the base and sides of the tin with baking paper.**

2. **Put the butter in a large saucepan and melt over the lowest heat for 5 minutes, then add both chocolates, the golden syrup and ground ginger and continue to melt over a low heat, stirring regularly (it's really important to keep the heat low here so that you don't burn the chocolate). When everything is melted and well combined, remove from the heat. Add the broken ginger biscuits, almonds, cranberries and marshmallows and mix until everything is totally combined.**

3. **Press the mixture firmly into the lined tin and lay the gingerbread men on top. Allow to set in the fridge for at least 3 hours.**

4. **Turn out of the tin and cut into small chunks using a very sharp knife.**

| MAKES 16 PIECES |
| --- |

**150g** unsalted butter
**250g** dark chocolate (50–55% cocoa solids), chopped
**150g** milk chocolate, chopped
**4 tbsp** golden syrup
**2 tsp** ground ginger
**150g** gingernut biscuits, crushed into chunks
**75g** flaked almonds
**100g** dried cranberries
**200g** mini marshmallows
**100g** mini gingerbread men, for the topping

**You will need:** 20cm square baking tin or dish

Store your rocky road in the fridge for up to 5 days.

If serving to vegetarians, make sure you use vegan marshmallows.

# HONEYCOMB

**15 MINS, PLUS COOLING TIME**

I generally avoid recipes that require a precise science, but I make an exception for this. The transformation of regular sugar into golden homemade honeycomb feels something like magic, it's such a treat to give and receive. You can, apparently, make it without a sugar thermometer but I have to say, I've never had a great deal of success and would highly recommend that if you plan on making this you do invest in one.

1. Line a baking tray with baking paper.

2. Put the golden syrup and caster sugar in a large saucepan and place over a medium heat. As they melt, stir them together, but once combined leave to heat without stirring.

3. Put your thermometer in the pan and when the mixture has reached 150°C, and is bubbling very hard, sprinkle over the bicarbonate of soda and take the pan off the heat.

4. You will need to work quickly here: beat the mixture until it starts to foam, then pour it onto the lined baking tray and leave for 1–2 hours to fully harden. Be careful, it will be VERY hot.

5. Cut or break into bite-sized pieces.

| SERVES 6 |
|---|

**150g** golden syrup
**400g** caster sugar
**1 tbsp** bicarbonate of soda

**You will need:** sugar thermometer

Store in an airtight container at room temperature (not in the fridge) for up to 1 week.

# SALTED CARAMEL TRUFFLES

**45 MINS, PLUS OVERNIGHT SETTING TIME**

Homemade truffles are such a decadent treat. I don't often have the patience to make and roll them myself, but I'm willing to make an exception at Christmastime. There is something slightly cathartic about peacefully rolling them for 20 minutes during this chaotic period. (Not to mention the fact that taste-testing is a chef's perk.)

1. Line the base and sides of a baking tin or dish with baking paper (if using). The tin or dish helps with portioning, but you can mould the truffles straight from the bowl if you prefer.

2. Put the finely chopped chocolate into a large microwaveable bowl and add the double cream. Microwave in 30-second bursts, mixing well after each burst, until the chocolate is completely melted. Alternatively, melt in a large heatproof bowl over a pan of simmering water (do not let the bottom of the bowl touch the water), stirring gently until melted.

3. Add the caramel and sea salt and mix well. The chocolate may look like it is splitting, but keep the faith and continue beating until you have a smooth mixture. Pour into the lined baking dish (if using) refrigerate overnight (or for at least 6 hours).

4. Remove the truffle mixture from the fridge, turn it out onto a chopping board and cut into 36 cubes. Use clean hands to roll each cube into a ball.

5. Put the icing sugar, cocoa and hazelnuts into three separate bowls, put 12 truffles in each bowl and gently shake until they are well coated. Store in the fridge.

## MAKES 36 TRUFFLES

**For the Truffles**
**400g** milk chocolate, finely chopped
**100ml** double cream
**200g** tinned caramel
(about half of a 397g tin)
**1 tsp** sea salt flakes

**To Decorate**
**30g** icing sugar, sifted
**20g** good-quality cocoa powder, sifted
**50g** chopped roasted hazelnuts
(you can buy these already roasted and chopped)

**You will need:** 20cm square baking tin or dish

Store in a container in the fridge (if you didn't eat them all accidentally first) for up to 1 week.

# HOT CHOCOLATE JARS

**10 MINS**

This is a really simple, no cooking required, homemade gift. The hot chocolate it makes is rich and delicious. This mixture will fill a container about the size of a jam jar. If it doesn't come quite to the top add more marshmallows so it's packed tightly.

1. Mix the cocoa and sugar together until well combined, spoon into the bottom of a jar and level out. Add a layer of the chopped chocolate and level it out. Finish with a layer of the marshmallows to fill the jar.

2. Pop the lid on and add a ribbon and instruction label.

---

### SERVES 4

**For a jar for 4 people**
**30g** good-quality cocoa powder
**20g** caster sugar
**60g** dark chocolate (about 70% cocoa solid), roughly chopped
**30g** mini marshmallows (vegetarian, if necessary)

**You will need:** medium jam jar

---

### TO MAKE AHEAD

Assemble jars up to 2 weeks in advance and store at room temperature.

---

If serving to vegetarians, make sure you use vegan marshmallows.

---

Here is the wording to add to your labels:

*To make hot chocolate for 4 people, tip the contents of the jar into a large saucepan and add 1 litre of milk. Heat over a medium heat, whisking continuously until warmed though and the chocolate has melted.*

# Bakes & Treats

Whether you're creating cakes for a tea party or gifting a tray of bakes to show someone how much they mean to you, here are a selection of my favourite festive treats.

# CRANBERRY & ORANGE COOKIES

**30 MINUTES, PLUS FREEZING AND COOLING TIME**

I love to have a big batch of these in the freezer over the festive period. Prep the uncooked dough balls and they are ready to pull out and cook straight from frozen whenever the need for freshly baked cookies strikes you (which for me, of course, is often). They also happen to make the kitchen smell divine!

1. **Preheat the oven to 180°C fan/200°C/Gas Mark 6 and line two baking trays with baking paper (if you only have one baking tray you can bake them in two batches).**

2. **Put all of the ingredients, but only half of the cranberries (reserve the other half), in a large mixing bowl and combine with a hand-held electric whisk or wooden spoon. The mixture will look crumbly, then will eventually start to come together into a dough. You can use clean hands here to help bring the dough together.**

3. **Using a spoon, scoop up some dough, then use your hands to roll the dough into a ball. Continue scooping and rolling, to make 12 even-sized balls of the cookie mixture. Place them on the lined baking trays, making sure they are evenly spaced apart to allow room for spreading.**

4. **Squash the balls down slightly with your hands and press the remaining cranberries into the tops of the cookies. Freeze the balls on the baking tray for about 30 minutes before baking. (I really recommend this! It stops them spreading and losing their shape as they cook.)**

5. **Bake in the oven for 15–18 minutes until just golden at the edges.**

6. **Remove from the oven and leave to cool for about 30 minutes on the baking trays before moving.**

## MAKES 12 COOKIES

**50g** unsalted butter,
  at room temperature
**75g** caster sugar
**75g** soft light brown sugar
**1** egg
**250g** plain flour
**½ tsp** bicarbonate of soda
**½ tsp** baking powder
**2** oranges, zested
**200g** dried cranberries

## TO MAKE AHEAD

Make these up to the end of step 4. Freeze them for 1 hour, open, on the baking trays in the freezer, then remove from the baking trays and store the unbaked cookies in a freezer-safe container. When you're ready to bake, put the frozen raw cookies onto a baking tray, with plenty of space between each one, and bake for 25–30 minutes. Cool on the baking tray.

# GINGERBREAD LATTE LAYER CAKE

**1 HOUR, PLUS COOLING TIME**

If you're a fan of the festive coffee shop offerings at this time of year, here is one of those favourite flavours, but in a cake! It makes a delicious alternative to a traditional Christmas cake. You can also bake the sponge well ahead and freeze it.

1. **Preheat the oven to 180°C fan/200°C/Gas Mark 6. Grease the sandwich tins with butter and line the bases with baking paper.**

2. **Cream the butter and sugar until pale, light and fluffy with a hand-held electric whisk (if you have one) or a wooden spoon. Add the eggs one at a time, beating well after each addition. Don't worry if it starts to look a bit curdled, it'll all come together. Add the flour and ginger and mix to combine. If you've been using an electric whisk, do this bit by hand. It helps to keep the sponge light. Stir in the coffee and water mixture.**

3. **Divide the batter evenly between the prepared tins and smooth out with the back of a spoon. Make a bit of a dip in the middle of each sponge to account for rising, to help keep them level. Bake in the oven for about 25–35 minutes, or until a skewer inserted into the middle of each cake comes out clean. Remove from the oven and allow the cakes to cool in the tins for 5 minutes, then remove from the tins and allow to cool completely on a wire rack.**

4. **While the cakes cool, make the buttercream icing. Beat the butter in a bowl until pale, light and fluffy (use a hand-held electric whisk if you have one). Gradually sift in the icing sugar and ginger, mixing as you add it. Beat in a little boiling water to soften and lighten the texture of the icing (it should be light and fluffy).**

5. **When your cakes are completely cold, sandwich together with half of the buttercream (use a piping bag if you have one). Spread or pipe the remaining icing on top before sprinkling with gingerbread-man decorations.**

| SERVES 12 |
| --- |

**For the Cake**
**225g** unsalted butter, at room temperature, plus extra for greasing
**225g** caster sugar
**4 eggs**
**225g** self-raising flour
**1 tbsp** ground ginger
**1 tbsp** instant coffee granules dissolved in 50ml boiling water

**To Decorate**
**175g** unsalted butter, at room temperature
**300g** icing sugar
**2 tsp** ground ginger
**2–3 tsp** boiling water
edible gingerbread-man decorations

**You will need:** 2 x 18cm round sandwich tins, piping bag (if you have one)

**TO MAKE AHEAD**

When the sponges are completely cold, wrap them (un-iced) in a double layer of cling film. Store in the freezer for up to 3 months, until you're ready to use. Defrost at room temperature and then decorate.

You can find gingerbread-man sprinkles and edible decorations online or in cake decorating shops. For piping, I use a Wilton 1M nozzle.

# TRIPLE CHOCOLATE LOG

**1 HOUR 30 MINUTES, PLUS CHILLING TIME**

This is my version of the classic chocolate log, Bûche De Noël. This recipe isn't my most fuss free – it is a little labour of love – but it's really just three components and I've simplified it wherever possible. It would make a fun Sunday afternoon Christmas baking project and it's the perfect treat to bring out on Christmas evening. It's almost impossible to totally avoid the sponge cracking a little as you roll the log up, but don't worry, that's what icing is for! Slather it on and nobody will know.

**Make the ganache icing:**

1. **Put the finely chopped chocolate into a heatproof bowl and set aside.**

2. **Put the double cream into a small saucepan over a medium heat on the hob and heat until it is bubbling on the surface. Remove the cream from the heat and pour over the chocolate in the bowl. Allow to sit for 5 minutes.**

3. **Beat the cream and chocolate together until smooth. Leave at room temperature, uncovered, in a cool part of your kitchen.**

**Make the filling:**

4. **Melt the white chocolate: You can either heat in the microwave for 30 seconds, then mix for 30 seconds and repeat until melted (be sure to mix very well every 30 seconds even if it doesn't look like it needs it). OR you can melt it in a small heatproof bowl, over a pan of simmering water (do not let the bowl touch the water!). Set aside for 5 minutes until it's room temperature.**

5. **Once the chocolate is cool, put the cream, cream cheese and chocolate into a large bowl and whisk until it forms stiff peaks. Put in the fridge while you make the sponge.**

**Make the sponge:**

6. **Preheat the oven to 180°C fan/200°C/Gas Mark 6. Line the baking tin with baking parchment or baking paper (not greaseproof paper). Press the paper right into the edges.**

**SERVES 12**

**For the Ganache**
**350g** dark chocolate (about 50% cocoa solids), very finely chopped
**350ml** double cream

**For the Filling**
**100g** white chocolate
**150ml** double cream
**150g** full-fat cream cheese
**100g** raspberry jam

**For the Sponge**
**8** eggs, separated
**200g** light soft brown sugar
**60g** cocoa powder
**2 tbsp** caster sugar

**To Decorate**
fresh raspberries and blackberries
sprigs of holly (berries removed and discarded)

**You will need:** 30 x 38cm baking tin

**TO MAKE AHEAD**
Make and store in the fridge for up to 24 hours before serving.

7. Put the egg yolks in a food mixer and whisk for a couple of minutes. Sprinkle over the soft brown sugar, breaking up any lumps, and whisk until you have a thick mixture. Sift in the cocoa and continue to whisk until completely combined.

8. In a clean bowl, whip up the egg whites to soft peaks. Tip about a third of the egg whites into the chocolate yolk mixture and beat with a spoon until fully combined (this loosens the mixture slightly so it's easier to fold into the rest of the egg whites).

9. Now tip that chocolate yolk mixture into the bowl with the remaining whites. Fold everything carefully together with a spoon, trying not to knock the air out. Pour this into the tin and spread out evenly. Bake for 25–30 minutes until the top is dry and bouncy when pressed with your finger. Remove from the oven and set aside to cool for 5 minutes.

10. Lay a fresh sheet of baking paper on your work surface, larger than the cake, and sprinkle over the caster sugar. Carefully lift the baking paper underneath the cake, so you take it off its baking tray, and flip it over onto the caster sugar. The top of your sponge is now sitting on top of the caster sugar and the bottom of your sponge, covered in the baking paper it cooked on, is facing upwards.

11. We are now going to roll this up, while it's still warm. (If it's too hot to handle, leave it for 5 minutes, but you must roll it while it's still warm; this avoids it cracking later.) Leave both sheets of baking paper in situ and roll up THE LONG SIDE of the cake, using the baking paper to help you; it doesn't need to be too tight or too neat. You'll end up with a long, thin roll shape. Set aside to cool for 1 hour.

12. While the sponge is cooling, check on the ganache. Depending on how warm your kitchen is, the setting time can vary a lot. If it is a scoopable, spreadable texture now, continue to leave at room temperature. If it's still quite runny, put it in the fridge while the sponge cools, to firm up.

To assemble:

13. When the sponge is fully cold, carefully unroll it and peel the baking paper off the sides. Gently open out the rolled sponge just enough to be able to add the filling. Spoon on the raspberry jam and smooth it all over the surface.

14. Spoon the white chocolate cream on top and carefully smooth out. It is helpful if you leave a gap of about 3cm along one long edge, which will be the end of your roll – this helps it to be less messy when you roll it up!

15. Roll the sponge back up, complete with the filling, following the same rolling as before. You should have a long, filled log. Now, use a sharp knife to cut about a quarter of the log off, at an angle, and reposition it against the side of the log. Sit the whole thing on a chopping board or covered tray.

16. Check on your ganache; give it a good stir to check it is smooth and spreadable (if not, and it's still too runny, put back into the fridge for more time until it's thickened up). Spread or pipe the ganache all over the log. Use a fork to make 'log' patterns and decorate with berries and some holly to add to the woodland theme! Keep it stored in the fridge.

# SPICED CHRISTMAS CUPCAKES

**25 MINS, PLUS COOLING TIME**

We all need a great Christmas cupcake recipe: they're good for an easy baking project with children or for taking to a party to impress. I pipe these simply with green icing to give something like the impression of a Christmas tree. You can buy gel food colouring in most supermarkets now, or buy online. Avoid liquid food colouring as it will make the icing too runny.

1.  **Preheat the oven to 180°C fan/200°C/Gas Mark 6 and line the tin with cupcake cases.**

2.  **Cream the butter and sugar in a bowl until pale, light and fluffy (use a hand-held electric whisk if you have one). Beat in the eggs, one at a time, mixing well after each addition. Don't worry if it curdles slightly, it will come good. Mix in the flour, cocoa, mixed spice and milk – do this by hand (if you've been using an electric whisk) as it helps to keep the cakes light.**

3.  **Divide the mixture evenly among the cases – I use an ice cream scoop as this gives the perfect amount and ensures some uniformity – and bake in the oven for 15 minutes, until golden and slightly bouncy to the touch.**

4.  **Meanwhile, make the icing. Beat the butter in a bowl until pale, light and fluffy, then beat in the icing sugar gradually. If the icing is too stiff, add a teaspoon or two of boiling water to soften it. Mix in the food colouring.**

5.  **Remove the cupcakes from the oven, carefully take them out of the tin and place on a wire rack to cool for at least 30 minutes.**

6.  **When the cakes are completely cold, transfer your icing to a piping bag fitted with a star nozzle (I like a Wilton 1M nozzle). Pipe swirls on the cupcakes to resemble Christmas trees and add sprinkles.**

You need to use gel food colouring, not liquid (which makes the icing too runny). You can buy gel colouring online, in some supermarkets, or in cake decorating shops. They vary a lot in strength so add a tiny bit at a time until you get the colour you want.

## MAKES 12 CUPCAKES

**For the Cupcakes**
**200g** unsalted butter, at room temperature
**200g** caster sugar
**4** eggs
**160g** self-raising flour
**40g** good-quality cocoa powder
**1 tbsp** mixed spice
**5 tbsp** semi-skimmed milk

**To Decorate**
**250g** unsalted butter, at room temperature
**500g** icing sugar, sifted
green gel food colouring (see Note)
edible Christmas sprinkles

**You will need:** 12-hole cupcake/muffin tin and 12 cupcake cases, piping bag fitted with star nozzle (if you have one)

### TO MAKE AHEAD

Bake the cakes and when they are completely cold wrap (un-iced) in a double layer of cling film. Store in the freezer for up to 3 months. Defrost at room temperature and then decorate.

# PUFF PASTRY MINCE PIE SWIRLS

**25 MINS**

Meet my mince pie for mince pie haters. These are fun to make, there's no faffing with crimping the edges of a mince pie, but they are every bit as delicious. Assemble them in advance and freeze if you'd like to keep some ready for any urgent need for baked goods!

1. **Preheat the oven to 180°C fan/200°C/Gas Mark 6 and line a baking tray with baking paper (not greaseproof paper).**

2. **Unroll the puff pastry sheet and spread the mincemeat all over the surface. Position a short end of the rectangle of pastry nearest you, then roll it up so that the spread is on the inside. Use a sharp knife to cut the roll in half, in half again and so on until you end up with 8 equal-sized pieces. Wiping the knife clean between each cut will help to keep the swirls looking neat.**

3. **Place the pastries, swirl side up, on the lined baking tray and brush the tops and sides with the beaten egg. Sprinkle a few flaked almonds on top of each one and bake for 18–20 minutes or until golden all over.**

4. **Remove from the oven and leave to cool on a wire rack.**

## MAKES 8 SWIRLS

**320g** ready-rolled puff pastry sheet
**250g** mincemeat
**1** egg, beaten
**25g** flaked almonds

## TO MAKE AHEAD

Prepare the swirls up to step 3, placing them on the tray but not brushing the tops or sprinkling them with flaked almonds. Freeze the raw swirls for 1 hour, open, on the tray in the freezer, then remove and store in a freezer-safe container for up to 3 months. When you're ready to bake, put the swirls onto a baking tray, brush with beaten egg, top with almonds and bakefor 25–30 minutes.

# SLOW COOKER
# SPICED HOT CHOCOLATE

## 1 HOUR 10 MINS

Whether you're coming in from a cold walk or cosying up for a movie afternoon, hot chocolate is always a warming winter treat. This version can cook away slowly in the slow cooker (or make it on the hob) while the festive spices infuse. Serve piled with marshmallows, of course.

1. **Mix the cocoa powder in a small bowl or mug with enough of the milk to make a smooth paste. Add this paste along with all of the other ingredients to the slow cooker (except the mini marshmallows) and mix until there are no lumps of cocoa paste. Put the lid on and cook on HIGH for 1–2 hours, stirring occasionally, or until the hot chocolate is thick and smooth.**

2. **Serve in mugs with marshmallows on top.**

### TO MAKE WITHOUT A SLOW COOKER

Put everything (except the marshmallows) in a large saucepan and cook over a low heat, stirring occasionally, for 15–20 minutes until the hot chocolate is thick and smooth.

| SERVES 6 |
| --- |

**30g** good-quality cocoa powder
**1 litre** whole milk
**300ml** single cream
**200g** milk chocolate,
   broken into small pieces
**3** cinnamon sticks
**1 tsp** ground ginger
**¼** nutmeg, grated

**To Serve**
mini marshmallows (vegetarian,
   if necessary)

If serving to vegetarians, make sure you use vegan marshmallows.

# THE CHRISTMAS CAKE RECIPE

**5 HOURS, PLUS DECORATING TIME**

I've made many Christmas cakes over the years, with plenty of failures among them! My main piece of advice is to cook the cake very slowly, at a very low temperature. Don't be tempted to rush it. You'll be rewarded by a tender, dense, rich cake that lasts well beyond the Christmas festivities. Ideally a Christmas cake should be made two or three months before Christmas and be 'fed' regularly with brandy, however, we've tested this one after just a month and it's still delicious.

1. **Put the fruit, brandy, orange zest and juice into a large bowl and mix well. Either leave to soak overnight covered with cling film OR put in a microwavable bowl and microwave for 5 minutes until the fruit has softened and some of the liquid has been absorbed, then set aside for 1 hour to cool.**

2. **Line the base and sides of the inside of the cake tin with baking paper, then line the outside too. Do this by taking another sheet of baking paper twice the height of your tin, fold it in half and wrap it around the outside and secure it tightly with some string.**

3. **When you're ready to make the cake, preheat the oven to 120°C fan/140°C/Gas Mark 1.**

4. **In a large bow,l mix the soaked fruit and liquid, eggs, flour, baking powder, butter, treacle, cinnamon, ground ginger, sugar and almonds. If you have a hand-held electric whisk you can use it here. Beat well until the mixture is combined and there are no pockets of flour remaining.**

5. **Pour the cake mixture into your lined tin and smooth the top so it is level. Put the cake into the oven on the lowest shelf and bake for 3 hours. After this time, test the cake by inserting a skewer into the middle – if any cake mixture remains on the skewer, bake for a little longer. It may take up to 3½ hours to cook. The top of the cake should look dry and be an even, golden colour.**

6. **Remove the cake from the oven and leave to cool in the tin. When the cake is cold, remove from the tin, peel off the baking paper it was cooked in and wrap well in baking paper. »**

**MAKES 16 PIECES**

**600g** dried mixed fruit
**150ml** brandy, plus extra for feeding the cake afterwards
**2** oranges, zested and juiced
**3** eggs
**150g** plain flour
**1 tsp** baking powder
**185g** unsalted butter, at room temperature
**35g** black treacle
**1 tsp** ground cinnamon
**1 tsp** ground ginger
**150g** soft light brown sugar
**75g** flaked almonds

**You will need:** 18cm round loose-bottomed cake tin (the type with deep sides)

Store your cake in an airtight container in the cupboard for at least 1 month and preferably 3 months.

You can replace the soaking brandy with apple juice (and do not feed the cake) if you prefer an alcohol-free version.

# THE CHRISTMAS CAKE RECIPE

## HOW TO FEED YOUR CAKE

1. Make several holes in your cake using a metal skewer and pour over 1 tablespoon of brandy each week for 4 weeks.

## HOW TO ICE AND DECORATE YOUR CAKE

1. Heat the apricot jam carefully in the microwave or in a pan over a low heat. If your jam has lumps of fruit in, you may need to pass it through a sieve.

2. Use a pastry brush to cover all sides and the top of the cake with the jam.

3. Knead the marzipan with clean hands until it is pliable. Place the marzipan ball between two sheets of cling film and roll it out using a rolling pin. Check as you roll that it is wide enough to cover the cake.

4. Gently place the marzipan on the cake, use your hands to gently smooth the marzipan over the cake – trim any excess at the edges. If you have time, allow the marzipan to dry for 24 hours before icing your cake (you could ice immediately but, if wet, the colour of the marzipan can come through the icing and discolour it).

5. When you're ready to ice the cake, take the icing out of the packet and knead it with very clean hands (don't wear a fluffy jumper!) until it is smooth and pliable.

6. Sprinkle the icing sugar on to a clean work surface and a rolling pin. Roll out the icing until it is wide enough to cover the cake.

**To Decorate**
**75g** apricot jam (smooth if you can find it)
**900g** ready-made marzipan
**750g** ready-made sugar paste
   or fondant icing
icing sugar
green and red gel food colouring
ribbon

**You will need:** rolling pin and holly cutters

7. Brush the surface of the cake with cool boiled water and gently place the icing over the cake, smoothing it with your hands. Trim away any excess icing (keep the offcuts).

8. Take the icing offcuts and use green gel food colouring to make a couple of shades of green icing.

9. Use the red gel food colouring to colour a very small amount of the icing red.

10. Roll the green icings out (sieved icing sugar can help here, but try to only use it on the underside, or a very small amount on top, or your holly will look 'dusty').

11. Cut out mixed sizes and shapes of holly leaves. Roll some tiny berries from the red fondant. Using a small brush, or clean finger, dab a little water onto the cake to 'glue' them on in a wreath shape.

12. Trim the bottom edge of the cake with ribbon (secure with a pin or Sellotape at the back).

Be sure to use gel food colouring, not liquid.

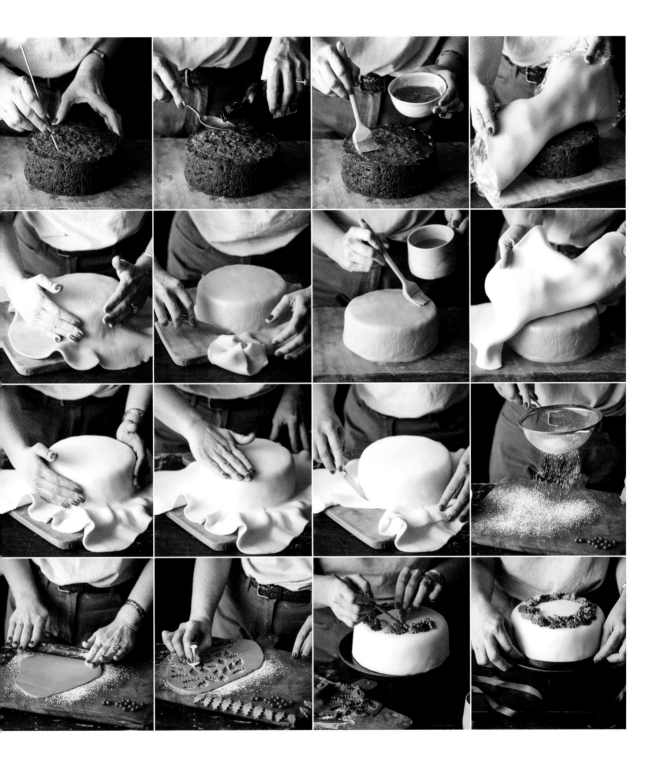

# DIETARY ADAPTIONS

This table is suggested as a guide only for how to adapt recipes to suit different diets. Please be sure to thoroughly check all individual ingredients before including. Particularly for allergies, check, check and check again before cooking.

We have tested gluten-free recipes with 'Freee' brand gluten-free flour unless otherwise stated. Other flours will vary.

Please always ensure the stock cubes you are using are suitable for your dietary needs.

For vegetarian or vegan mentions including cheese, we have assumed using a suitable cheese or cheese alternative.

These adaptions will alter the nutritional information on pages 214–17.

| | GLUTEN FREE | DAIRY FREE | VEGAN | VEGETARIAN | NUT FREE |
|---|---|---|---|---|---|
| **CLASSIC ROAST TURKEY WITH HERB BUTTER** | Suitable | Use plant-based block butter | Not suitable | Not suitable | Suitable |
| **SLOW COOKER TURKEY & GRAVY** | Use gluten-free soy sauce | Suitable | Not suitable | Not suitable | Suitable |
| **SLOW COOKER ROAST BEEF** | Replace plain flour with cornflour | Suitable | Not suitable | Not Suitable | Suitable |
| **MUSHROOM WELLINGTONS** | Use gluten-free pastry | Use plant-based puff pastry, cheese and butter | Use plant-based puff pastry, cheese and butter | Suitable | Suitable |
| **RIDICULOUSLY DELICIOUS NUT ROAST** | Use gluten-free panko breadcrumbs | Suitable | Suitable | Suitable | Not suitable |
| **ORANGE & HONEY GLAZED SALMON** | Suitable | Suitable | Not suitable | Not suitable | Suitable |
| **ROAST TURKEY TRAYBAKE** | Use gluten-free sausages | Suitable | Not suitable | Not suitable | Suitable |
| **PIGS IN BLANKETS** | Use gluten-free sausages | Suitable | Not suitable | Not suitable | Suitable |
| **STRESS-FREE ROAST POTATOES** | Suitable | Suitable | Suitable | Suitable | Suitable |
| **GLAZED CARROTS & PARSNIPS** | Suitable | Suitable | Use adaptions in the recipe | Suitable | Suitable |

| | GLUTEN FREE | DAIRY FREE | VEGAN | VEGETARIAN | NUT FREE |
|---|---|---|---|---|---|
| **FESTIVE BRUSSELS SPROUTS** | Suitable | Suitable | Use adaptions in the recipe | Use adaptions in the recipe | Omit the nuts |
| **BRAISED RED CABBAGE** | Suitable | Use plant-based spread | Use plant-based spread | Suitable | Suitable |
| **CAULIFLOWER CHEESE** | Suitable | Not suitable | Not suitable | Suitable | Suitable |
| **YORKSHIRE PUDDINGS** | Replace flour with cornflour. They may take a little longer to cook | Use plant-based milk alternative. They may take a little longer to cook | Not suitable | Suitable | Suitable |
| **SAUSAGE & APRICOT STUFFING** | Use gluten-free panko breadcrumbs | Use plant-based spread | Not suitable | Not suitable | Omit the nuts |
| **SAGE & ONION STUFFING BALLS** | Use gluten-free panko breadcrumbs | Suitable | Suitable | Suitable | Suitable |
| **MAKE-AHEAD GRAVY** | Use gluten-free soy sauce | Suitable | Check that the alcohol you are using is suitable for vegans | Check that the alcohol you are using is suitable for vegetarians | Suitable |
| **CRANBERRY SAUCE** | Suitable | Suitable | Suitable | Suitable | Suitable |
| **BREAD SAUCE** | Use gluten-free breadcrumbs | Use plant-based milk and cream alternatives | Use plant-based milk and cream alternatives | Suitable | Suitable |
| **PRAWN COCKTAIL CUPS** | Use Henderson's Relish | Use a plant-based mayonnaise | Not suitable | Not suitable | Suitable |
| **SMOKED SALMON CANAPES** | Use gluten-free bread | Use plant-based crème fraiche | Not suitable | Not suitable | Suitable |
| **BRIE & CRANBERRY BITES** | Use gluten-free puff pastry | Not suitable | Not suitable | Suitable | Suitable |
| **BAKED CAMEMBERT** | Suitable | Not suitable | Not suitable | Not suitable | Omit the nuts |
| **GOAT'S CHEESE BITES** | Use gluten-free bread | Not suitable | Not suitable | Suitable | Omit the nuts |
| **SMASHED PEA CROSTINI** | Use gluten-free bread | Suitable | Suitable | Suitable | Not suitable |

| | GLUTEN FREE | DAIRY FREE | VEGAN | VEGETARIAN | NUT FREE |
|---|---|---|---|---|---|
| **PALMA HAM & MELON BITES** | Suitable | Suitable | Not suitable | Not suitable | Suitable |
| **HONEY MUSTARD SAUSAGES** | Use gluten-free sausages | Suitable | Not suitable | Not suitable | Suitable |
| **CHRISTMAS MORNING MUFFINS** | Replace flour with gluten-free plain flour and add 2 tsp of gluten-free baking powder | Use plant-based milk alternative | Not suitable | Suitable | Suitable |
| **CHRISTMAS GRANOLA** | Use gluten-free oats | Suitable | Replace egg white with 2 tbsp aqua faba (the liquid from a tin of chickpeas) and replace honey with maple syrup | Suitable | Omit the nuts |
| **HASH BROWN BREAKFAST BAKE** | Use gluten-free hash browns | Use plant-based milk and cheese alternatives | Not suitable | Omit the bacon | Suitable |
| **CHRISTMAS MORNING COCKTAIL CUBES** | Suitable | Suitable | Check that the alcohol you are using is suitable for vegans | Check that the alcohol you are using is suitable for vegetarians | Suitable |
| **CHRISTMAS TREE FRUIT SALAD** | Suitable | Suitable | Not suitable | Not suitable | Suitable |
| **CROISSANT CHRISTMAS TREE** | Use gluten-free pastry | Not suitable | Not suitable | Suitable | Use nut-free chocolate spread |
| **SLOW COOKER ROASTED GAMMON** | Suitable | Suitable | Not suitable | Not suitable | Suitable |
| **SLOW COOKER VEGETABLE & CASHEW CURRY** | Suitable | Suitable | Suitable | Suitable | Omit the nuts. |
| **FESTIVE BRAISED BEEF** | Replace flour with gluten-free flour | Suitable | Not suitable | Not suitable | Suitable |
| **SLOW COOKER MOROCCAN-STYLE CHICKEN STEW** | Suitable | Suitable | Not suitable | Not suitable | Omit the nuts |
| **ROASTED WINTER SALAD** | Suitable | Omit the cheese | Omit the feta and replace honey with maple syrup | Suitable | Omit the nuts |

| | GLUTEN FREE | DAIRY FREE | VEGAN | VEGETARIAN | NUT FREE |
|---|---|---|---|---|---|
| **CHEESE & TOMATO TART** | Use gluten-free pastry | Use plant-based pastry, pesto and cream cheese | Use plant-based pastry, pesto and cream cheese | Suitable | Use nut-free pesto |
| **CHRISTMAS COLESLAW** | Suitable | Use plant-based mayonnaise and yoghurt alternatives | Use plant-based mayonnaise and yoghurt alternatives | Suitable | Suitable |
| **CAPRESE-STYLE PASTA SALAD** | Use gluten-free pasta | Use plant-based pesto and omit the cheese | Use plant-based pesto and omit the cheese | Suitable | Use nut-free pesto and omit the nuts |
| **CREAMY POTATO GRATIN** | Suitable | Use plant-based milk and cream alternatives | Use plant-based milk and cream alternatives | Suitable | Suitable |
| **PIGS IN BLANKETS SAUSAGE ROLLS** | Use gluten-free sausages and puff pastry | Use plant-based puff pastry | Not suitable | Not suitable | Suitable |
| **SLOW COOKER MULLED WINE** | Suitable | Suitable | Check that the alcohol you are using is suitable for vegans | Check that the alcohol you are using is suitable for vegetarians | Suitable |
| **DOUGHBALL PLATTER** | Use a gluten-free bread mix or dough | Use plant-based block butter | Use plant-based block butter | Suitable | Suitable |
| **LEFTOVER TURKEY CURRY** | Suitable | Suitable | Not suitable | Not suitable | Suitable |
| **CHEESE & CHUTNEY SCONES** | Replace flour and baking powder with gluten-free versions | Not suitable | Not suitable | Suitable | Suitable |
| **BOXING DAY FRITTATA** | Suitable | Omit the cheese | Not suitable | Suitable | Use nut-free pesto |
| **ONE-POT BOXING DAY PIE** | Use gluten-free pastry | Use a plant-based puff pastry and plant-based milk alternatives | Omit the meat and use additonal leftover vegetables, plant-based puff pastry and plant-based milk alternatives | Omit the meat and use additonal leftover vegetables | Suitable |
| **LEFTOVER ROOT VEGETABLE SOUP** | Suitable | Use plant-based cream | Use plant-based cream | Suitable | Suitable |
| **CHOCOLATE SALAMI** | Use gluten-free biscuits | Use dairy-free chocolate and plant-based block butter | Use dairy-free chocolate and plant-based block butter | Suitable | Replace nuts with more dried fruit and/or biscuits |

| | GLUTEN FREE | DAIRY FREE | VEGAN | VEGETARIAN | NUT FREE |
|---|---|---|---|---|---|
| **CHRISTMAS BROWNIES** | Replace flour with gluten-free flour | Not suitable | Not suitable | Suitable | Omit the nuts |
| **WREATH PAVLOVA** | Suitable | Not suitable | Not suitable | Suitable | Suitable |
| **ZESTY LEMON POTS** | Suitable | Not suitable | Not suitable | Suitable | Not suitable |
| **SLOW COOKER CHOCOLATE ORANGE PUDDING** | Replace flour and baking powder with gluten-free versions | Use plant-based spread | Not suitable | Suitable | Suitable |
| **VERY BERRY TRIFLE** | Replace swiss roll with gluten-free alternative | Not suitable | Not suitable | Check that the jelly you are using is suitable for vegetarians | Omit the nuts |
| **VEGAN BLACK FOREST TART** | Use gluten-free biscuits for the base | Suitable | Suitable | Suitable | Suitable |
| **NO-BAKE CHOCO-NUT CHEESECAKE** | Use gluten-free biscuits and chocolates | Not suitable | Not suitable | Suitable | Use nut-free chocolates |
| **CHRISTMAS TIRAMISU** | Replace panettone with gluten-free alternative | Not suitable | Not suitable | Suitable | Suitable |
| **CHRISTMAS POPCORN SLAB** | Suitable | Suitable | Suitable | Suitable | Suitable |
| **PESTO PARMESAN STRAWS** | Use gluten-free pastry | Use plant-based puff pastry | Use plant-based puff pastry and pesto. Omit the cheese. Use a plant-based milk alternative to brush the pastry | Suitable | Use nut-free pesto |
| **SLOW COOKER RED ONION CHUTNEY** | Suitable | Suitable | Suitable | Suitable | Suitable |
| **GINGERBREAD ROCKY ROAD** | Use gluten-free biscuits | Use plant-based spread and dairy-free chocolate | Use plant-based spread, vegan marshmallows and dairy-free chocolate | Use vegan marshmallows | Omit the nuts |
| **HONEYCOMB** | Suitable | Suitable | Suitable | Suitable | Suitable |

| | GLUTEN FREE | DAIRY FREE | VEGAN | VEGETARIAN | NUT FREE |
|---|---|---|---|---|---|
| **CANDY CANE FUDGE** | Suitable | Use sweetened condensed coconut milk and dairy-free chocolate | Use sweetened condensed coconut milk and dairy-free chocolate | Suitable | Suitable |
| **HOT CHOCOLATE JARS** | Use gluten-free cocoa | Use dairy-free cocoa | Use dairy-free cocoa and vegan marshmallows | Use vegan marshmallows | Suitable |
| **SALTED CARAMEL TRUFFLES** | Use gluten-free cocoa | Not suitable | Not suitable | Suitable | Omit the nuts |
| **HOW TO MAKE A BRILLIANT CHEESEBOARD** | Check all ingredients are gluten-free | Use adaptions in the recipe | Use adaptions in the recipe | Use adaptions in the recipe | Check all ingredients are nut-free |
| **CRANBERRY & ORANGE COOKIES** | Use gluten-free flour | Use plant-based spread | Not suitable | Suitable | Suitable |
| **GINGERBREAD LATTE LAYER CAKE** | Not suitable | Not suitable | Not suitable | Suitable | Suitable |
| **SPICED CHRISTMAS CUPCAKES** | Replace flour with gluten-free flour | Use plant-based spread | Not suitable | Suitable | Suitable |
| **PUFF PASTRY MINCE PIE SWIRLS** | Use gluten-free pastry | Use a plant-based pastry, mincemeat and plant-based milk alternative to brush the pastry | Use a plant-based pastry, mincemeat and plant-based milk alternative to brush the pastry | Suitable | Use nut-free mincemeat |
| **SLOW COOKER SPICED HOT CHOCOLATE** | Use gluten-free cocoa | Use plant-based milk/cream and dairy-free chocolate. You may need to add some sugar as this may be quite bitter | Use plant-based milk/cream, vegan marshmallows and dairy-free chocolate. You may need to add some sugar as this may be quite bitter | Use vegan marshmallows | Suitable |
| **TRIPLE CHOCOLATE LOG** | Not suitable | Not suitable | Not suitable | Suitable | Suitable |
| **THE CHRISTMAS CAKE RECIPE** | Replace flour and baking powder with gluten-free versions | Use plant-based spread | Not suitable | Check that the alcohol you are using is suitable for vegetarians | Omit the nuts |

# NUTRITIONAL INFORMATION

Please use the nutritional information here as an approximate guide only. If you need exact measurements please confirm using your own branded ingredients. All measurements are per serving (as per the recipe page) unless otherwise stated. Where a recipe serving is variable (for example, 6–8 servings) the figures are always calculated per portion on the highest number of servings.

| | Energy<br>in kcals | Protein<br>in grams | Fat<br>in grams | Saturates<br>in grams | Carbs<br>in grams | Sugar<br>in grams | Fibre<br>in grams | Salt<br>in grams |
|---|---|---|---|---|---|---|---|---|
| **CLASSIC ROAST TURKEY WITH HERB BUTTER** (Per Serving) | 790 | 80.7 | 51.2 | 24.4 | 0.9g | 0.3 | 0.7 | 2.18 |
| **SLOW COOKER TURKEY & GRAVY** (Per Serving) | 394 | 84.8 | 5.3 | 1.8 | 1.6 | 0.3 | 0.5 | 1.02 |
| **SLOW COOKER ROAST BEEF** (Per Serving) | 586 | 52.8 | 35.0 | 13.9 | 13.3 | 5.4 | 2.9 | 1.11 |
| **MUSHROOM WELLINGTONS** (Per Serving) | 774 | 21.8 | 57.0 | 28.5 | 40.2 g | 6.4 | 7.3 | 1.5 |
| **RIDICULOUSLY DELICIOUS NUT ROAST** (Per Serving) | 536 | 18.2 | 34.4 | 5.3 | 34.4 | 15.6 | 8.1 | 1.10 |
| **ORANGE & HONEY GLAZED SALMON** (Per Serving) | 388 | 34.2 | 25.0 | 4.6 | 6.2 | 5.6 | 0.6 | 0.28 |
| **ROAST TURKEY TRAYBAKE** (Per Serving) | 701 | 50.2 | 38.1 | 14.2 | 34.8 | 10.5 | 9.0 | 2.34 |
| **PIGS IN BLANKETS** (Per Serving) | 258 | 10.6 | 21.0 | 7.4 | 5.5 | 1.7 | 1.7 | 1.36 |
| **STRESS-FREE ROAST POTATOES** (Per Serving) | 422 | 5.1 | 23.3 | 2.8 | 45.5 | 2.3 | 5.2 | 0.97 |
| **GLAZED CARROTS &X PARSNIPS** (Per Serving) | 311 | 3.3 | 11.3 | 1.5 | 44.1 | 35.4 | 10.0 | 0.26 |
| **FESTIVE BRUSSELS SPROUTS** (Per Serving) | 212 | 13.8 | 10.1 | 4.1 | 13.4 | 6.3 | 5.6 | 2.07 |
| **BRAISED RED CABBAGE** (Per Serving) | 216 | 2.1 | 8.4 | 5.0 | 29.3 | 28.1 | 6.2 | 0.12 |
| **CAULIFLOWER CHEESE** (Per Serving) | 217 | 14.5 | 11.3 | 6.9 | 13.5 | 7.4 | 2.2 | 0.69 |
| **YORKSHIRE PUDDINGS** (Per Pudding) | 93 | 3.7 | 4.1 | 0.9 | 10.1 | 0.9 | 0.5 | 0.13 |
| **SAUSAGE & APRICOT STUFFING** (Per Serving) | 353 | 11.2 | 22.8 | 9.2 | 23.5 | 9.1 | 4.3 | 1.08 |

| | Energy in kcals | Protein in grams | Fat in grams | Saturates in grams | Carbs in grams | Sugar in grams | Fibre in grams | Salt in grams |
|---|---|---|---|---|---|---|---|---|
| SAGE & ONION STUFFING BALLS *(Per Stuffing Ball)* | 87 | 1.5 | 5.0 | 2.4 | 8.8 | 1.4 | 0.6 | 0.50 |
| MAKE-AHEAD GRAVY *(Per Serving)* | 175 | 3.2 | 5.8 | 0.9 | 19.9 | 14.4 | 5.6 | 2.27 |
| CRANBERRY SAUCE *(Per Serving)* | 47 | 0.2 | 0.0 | 0.0 | 11.0 | 11.0 | 1.1 | 0.00 |
| BREAD SAUCE *(Per Serving)* | 98 | 3.1 | 4.6 | 2.8 | 10.6 | 4.0 | 0.6 | 0.23 |
| PRAWN COCKTAIL CUPS *(Per Serving)* | 162 | 8.4 | 13.0 | 1.0 | 2.5 | 2.3 | 0.5 | 0.93 |
| SMOKED SALMON CANAPÉS *(Per Serving)* | 350 | 10.2 | 27.1 | 16.2 | 15.0 | 2.0 | 2.5 | 1.37 |
| BRIE & CRANBERRY BITES *(Per Serving)* | 348 | 9.4 | 24.1 | 11.6 | 22.8 | 7.1 | 1.5 | 0.88 |
| BAKED CAMEMBERT *(Per Serving)* | 134 | 9.0 | 9.6 | 6.0 | 3.0 | 2.7 | 0.1 | 1.12 |
| GOAT'S CHEESE BITES *(Per Serving)* | 151 | 4.6 | 10.2 | 3.3 | 3.9 | 1.0 | 0.41 | |
| SMASHED PEA CROSTINI *(Per Serving)* | 362 | 10.8 | 18.5 | 3.1 | 36.1 | 4.0 | 3.7 | 0.71 |
| PARMA HAM & MELON BITES *(Per Serving)* | 111 | 8.5 | 5.0 | 1.4 | 6.4 | 6.4 | 2.9 | 0.16 |
| HONEY MUSTARD SAUSAGES *(Per Serving)* | 188 | 6.1 | 13.4 | 4.7 | 9.9 | 6.8 | 1.4 | 0.69 |
| CHRISTMAS MORNING MUFFINS *(Per Muffin)* | 185 | 3.4 | 9.3 | 1.5 | 21.2 | 6.1 | 1.7 | 0.40 |
| CHRISTMAS GRANOLA *(Per Serving)* | 311 | 6.8 | 15.7 | 1.5 | 33.0 | 13.3 | 5.5 | 0.05 |
| HASH BROWN BREAKFAST BAKE *(Per Serving)* | 379 | 23.3 | 18.3 | 7.3 | 28.8 | 3.3 | 3.4 | 0.88 |
| CHRISTMAS MORNING COCKTAIL CUBES *(Per Cube)* | 20 | 0.5 | 0.1 | 0.0 | 4.1 | 4.1 | 0.5 | 0.00 |
| CHRISTMAS TREE FRUIT SALAD *(Per Serving)* | 75 | 0.9 | 0.4 | 0.1 | 15.1 | 14.7 | 3.3 | 0.00 |
| CROISSANT CHRISTMAS TREE *(Per Serving)* | 435 | 7.2 | 23.5 | 17.5 | 45.4 | 22.5 | 3.3 | 0.08 |
| SLOW COOKER ROASTED GAMMON *(Per Serving)* | 431 | 44.4 | 19.2 | 6.3 | 19.2 | 18.5 | 1.4 | 5.51 |

| | Energy in kcals | Protein in grams | Fat in grams | Saturates in grams | Carbs in grams | Sugar in grams | Fibre in grams | Salt in grams |
|---|---|---|---|---|---|---|---|---|
| **SLOW COOKER VEGETABLE & CASHEW CURRY** (Per Serving) | 602 | 18.3 | 45.2 | 19.6 | 26.6 | 16.0 | 7.9 | 1.34 |
| **FESTIVE BRAISED BEEF** (Per Serving) | 677 | 69.5 | 35.6 | 13.3 | 17.8 | 10.2 | 3.0 | 1.86 |
| **SLOW COOKER MOROCCAN-STYLE CHICKEN STEW** (Per Serving) | 316 | 36.8 | 7.7 | 1.6 | 21.8 | 13.6 | 5.6 | 0.92 |
| **ROASTED WINTER SALAD** (Per Serving) | 379 | 5.4 | 21.5 | 4.2 | 36.9 | 31.6 | 6.4 | 1.08 |
| **CHEESE & TOMATO TART** (Per Serving) | 254 | 4.8 | 19.4 | 10.1 | 14.0 | 2.2 | 1.8 | 0.65 |
| **CHRISTMAS COLESLAW** (Per Serving) | 215 | 2.0 | 18.1 | 2.1 | 9.4 | 8.9 | 3.0 | 0.48 |
| **CAPRESE-STYLE PASTA SALAD** (Per Serving) | 391 | 13.5 | 23.0 | 7.0 | 30.9 | 5.3 | 2.2 | 0.71 |
| **CREAMY POTATO GRATIN** (Per Serving) | 371 | 5.6 | 21.8 | 13.5 | 36.2 | 4.1 | 3.8 | 0.22 |
| **PIGS IN BLANKETS SAUSAGE ROLLS** (Per Roll) | 236 | 8.1 | 16.6 | 6.8 | 12.8 | 2.9 | 1.7 | 0.67 |
| **MULLED WINE** (Per Serving) | 212 | 0.5 | 0.0 | 0.0 | 17.1 | 17.1 | 0.2 | 0.05 |
| **DOUGHBALL PLATTER** (Per Doughball) | 51 | 1.1 | 2.3 | 1.2 | 6.2 | 0.1 | 0.3 | 0.10 |
| **LEFTOVER TURKEY CURRY** (Per Serving) | 381 | 37.1 | 9.5 | 0.9 | 32.4 | 19.0 | 6.8 | 2.75 |
| **CHEESE & CHUTNEY SCONES** (Per Scone) | 438 | 14.7 | 19.7 | 11.8 | 49.1 | 2.8 | 2.6 | 1.86 |
| **BOXING DAY FRITTATA** (Per Serving) | 318 | 18.7 | 20.3 | 8.2 | 13.8 | 3.9 | 2.8 | 0.89 |
| **ONE-POT BOXING DAY PIE** (Per Serving) | 526 | 34.3 | 27.3 | 13.7 | 33.9 | 4.5 | 3.4 | 1.47 |
| **LEFTOVER ROOT VEGETABLE SOUP** (Per Serving) | 124 | 2.5 | 4.0 | 0.7 | 16.2 | 10.3 | 6.9 | 2.25 |
| **CHOCOLATE SALAMI** (Per Slice) | 287 | 4.2 | 19.9 | 10.2 | 21.9 | 17.9 | 1.7 | 0.34 |
| **CHRISTMAS BROWNIES** (Per Square) | 258 | 2.9 | 13.7 | 7.9 | 30.1 | 25.4 | 0.9 | 0.22 |
| **WREATH PAVLOVA** (Per Serving) | 347 | 3.0 | 18.0 | 11.1 | 42.2 | 42.2 | 2.1 | 0.10 |
| **ZESTY LEMON POTS** (Per Serving) | 864 | 2.4 | 74.8 | 46.5 | 45.3 | 45.3 | 0.3 | 0.08 |

| | Energy in kcals | Protein in grams | Fat in grams | Saturates in grams | Carbs in grams | Sugar in grams | Fibre in grams | Salt in grams |
|---|---|---|---|---|---|---|---|---|
| **SLOW COOKER CHOCOLATE ORANGE PUDDING** *(Per Serving)* | 521 | 9.5 | 22.6 | 13.2 | 68.2 | 44.9 | 3.8 | 0.60 |
| **VERY BERRY TRIFLE** *(Per Serving)* | 491 | 6.2 | 34.9 | 19.8 | 36.6 | 29.0 | 3.1 | 0.14 |
| **VEGAN BLACK FOREST TART** *(Per Serving)* | 277 | 1.8 | 19.8 | 4.9 | 22.7 | 12.7 | 0.9 | 0.34 |
| **NO BAKE CHOCO-NUT CHEESECAKE** *(Per Serving)* | 874 | 9.5 | 69.2 | 37.3 | 52.0 | 42.4 | 1.4 | 0.72 |
| **CHRISTMAS TIRAMISU** *(Per Serving)* | 626 | 6.7 | 50.3 | 31.5 | 34.4 | 23.9 | 1.0 | 0.32 |
| **CHRISTMAS POPCORN SLAB** *(Per Serving)* | 478 | 7.2 | 24.3 | 10.3 | 47.9 | 28.1 | 3.2 | 0.88 |
| **PESTO PARMESAN STRAWS** *(Per Straw)* | 109 | 3.3 | 7.7 | 3.6 | 6.2 | 0.4 | 0.6 | 0.30 |
| **SLOW COOKER RED ONION CHUTNEY** *(Per Serving)* | 17 | 0.2 | 0.0 | 0.0 | 3.7 | 3.3 | 0.4 | 0.00 |
| **GINGERBREAD ROCKY ROAD** *(Per Piece)* | 383 | 4.1 | 20.2 | 10.7 | 45.0 | 35.9 | 2.6 | 0.24 |
| **HONEYCOMB** *(Per Serving)* | 346 | 0.1 | 0.0 | 0.0 | 86.3 | 86.3 | 0.0 | 1.55 |
| **CANDY CANE FUDGE** *(Per Piece)* | 100 | 1.4 | 4.1 | 2.5 | 14.1 | 13.7 | 0.8 | 0.03 |
| **HOT CHOCOLATE JARS** *(Per Serving, Without Milk)* | 154 | 2.8 | 5.8 | 3.5 | 20.8 | 18.6 | 3.5 | 0.01 |
| **SALTED CARAMEL TRUFFLES** *(Per Serving)* | 101 | 1.5 | 6.0 | 3.2 | 9.9 | 9.8 | 0.5 | 0.19 |
| **CRANBERRY & ORANGE COOKIES** *(Per Cookie)* | 220 | 2.8 | 4.3 | 2.4 | 41.6 | 25.2 | 1.9 | 0.07 |
| **GINGERBREAD LATTE LAYER CAKE** *(Per Serving)* | 516 | 4.6 | 29.4 | 17.9 | 57.8 | 43.9 | 0.9 | 0.25 |
| **SPICED CHRISTMAS CUPCAKES** *(Per Cupcake)* | 599 | 5.0 | 33.5 | 20.5 | 68.6 | 58.3 | 1.7 | 0.22 |
| **PUFF PASTRY MINCE PIE SWIRLS** *(Per Serving)* | 277 | 4.2 | 14.3 | 5.4 | 32.0 | 20.2 | 1.5 | 0.38 |
| **SLOW COOKER SPICED HOT CHOCOLATE** *(Per Serving)* | 397 | 10.9 | 26.7 | 16.6 | 27.1 | 26.5 | 2.5 | 0.29 |
| **TRIPLE CHOCOLATE LOG** *(Per Serving)* | 592 | 9.6 | 39.4 | 22.9 | 47.9 | 46.9 | 3.7 | 0.32 |
| **THE CHRISTMAS CAKE RECIPE** *(Per Serving)* | 742 | 8.8 | 20.5 | 7.1 | 123.4 | 114.7 | 5.4 | 0.25 |

# INDEX

# ACKNOWLEDGEMENTS

Thank you, as always, for following me on social media, clicking on my website or telling your friends about my recipes. A special thanks if you are one of the 100,000 or so people who have used the Christmas Day plan on my website over the last couple of years. It's your glowing feedback that encouraged me to come up with What's for Christmas Dinner? and show my publisher how needed it is.

At Christmas, I often think about the people who work tirelessly to let the rest of us enjoy ourselves easily, safely, comfortably. If you're working supermarket shifts to keep us all fed, delivering our parcels to make our shopping easier, part of the emergency services keeping us safe or any other job that means the festive season doesn't look quite the same for you – THANK YOU, you're noticed and appreciated.

Writing this book has been such a treat, I never forget what a privilege it is to have a job I love and to work with a wonderful team (even when I made 13 chocolate logs in one month!).

**Pippa, Emma, Sam, Giz and Lydia –** thank you so much for your hard work and dedication to all aspects of the photography shoot, to make this book look so beautiful. You make it all feel so easy (even when trying to find a good-looking Christmas ham in April).

**Lydia and the HarperCollins team –** thank you for believing that the world needs an easier version of Christmas cooking and helping to make this book as brilliant as I knew it could be. Thanks to George, Sim, and everyone else involved behind the scenes; design, editorial, sales, publicity and marketing. So much work goes into a book that nobody sees and I'm very grateful that I get to do it with all of you.

**Laurie –** thanks for being the most supportive champion and an all-round brilliant person. Eating an entire cheeseboard for breakfast with you on the photoshoot will forever be a highlight.

**Debbie –** thank you as always for your tireless testing and brilliant feedback.

**Claire, Helen and Hattie –** thank you for all your work in the background, helping to keep everything going on the blog, while I wrote this book.

**Anna –** you're more brilliant than you will ever realise, and I notice and appreciate everything you do, every day. Thank you for helping to make work a total pleasure and for being so dedicated to these books.

And for **Dominic, George, Harriet, Imogen, Hattie, Hugo and Sophia**, who came into my life and made Christmas more magical than I could ever have imagined. Thank you.